The Choral Works
of Jennifer Higdon

The Choral Works of Jennifer Higdon:

Choral Kaleidoscope

By

William Skoog

Edited by Meagan Mason

Cambridge
Scholars
Publishing

The Choral Works of Jennifer Higdon: Choral Kaleidoscope

By William Skoog

This book first published 2021

Cambridge Scholars Publishing

Lady Stephenson Library, Newcastle upon Tyne, NE6 2PA, UK

British Library Cataloguing in Publication Data
A catalogue record for this book is available from the British Library

ISBN (10): 1-5275-6868-7
ISBN (13): 978-1-5275-6868-6

TABLE OF CONTENTS

ACKNOWLEDGEMENTS

It truly takes a village to write such a book. I am most grateful to Jennifer Higdon, a tremendous human being and an enormously gifted and inspired composer, who has written this music and has been so supportive in this project. I am grateful to all of the poets who have provided texts for these works, notably Jeanne Minahan for her enthusiasm and support. I am further grateful for the support and help of Cheryl Lawson, Jennifer's business partner, for the tremendous amount of administrative help and assistance, from providing scores and recordings to offering feedback on the manuscript. To Jennifer and Cheryl, my thankfulness for their belief in me, in my work, and profound trust in my insights to present their art.

I am grateful to Gretchen Steiner, a dear friend for many years and an amazing work partner and colleague in this process, who has edited my (all too many) words and created and formatted all the many musical figures contained in this book, raising questions about them, editing them, cleaning them up for publication, and editing several more that were ultimately discarded. Her countless hours of work and dedication and her patience with me in this process and care for this project cannot be overstated.

I am grateful to Meagan Mason, an editorial warrior, who has educated me to write more succinctly and clearly—or at least, to write more proficiently and with better skill. Meagan, a skilled and trained musician, has challenged every theoretical and analytical thought to better serve Jennifer's music and helped me develop an even more critical eye for writing music analyses. Meagan has been a godsend in this process.

Many colleagues from Rhodes College deserve hearty thanks: Dr. Vanessa Rogers, musicologist, for reading a first draft and propelling me from writing an article to writing this important manuscript. Without Vanessa's encouragement, this would not have happened. To Dr. Evan Williams, Professor of Composition and Orchestra, for applicable, contemporary theoretical concepts; to Dr. Carole Blankenship, Chair of Music, for her support and encouragement; to Dr. Brian Shaffer, former Associate Dean of Academic Affairs; and Dr. Milton Moreland, former Provost at Rhodes; to Dr. Michael Drompp, former Dean of Academic Affairs; and Dr. Timothy Huebner, Associate Provost, who inspired me and supported this project through its completion. In ways more than I can enumerate, all of these people helped this book come to life.

Finally, to my wife, Elaine, who prompted me to start this process and encouraged me throughout this trial by fire. Elaine urged me, against my own insecurities as a writer to doggedly pursue this over these last several years, making it and keeping it a priority. Believing in me, believing moreover in Jennifer and her music, and supporting me without wavering, she is not only my wife, but my best, dedicated friend and champion of any of my work on or off the podium. I call her my amazing Elaine, and she is. I dedicate this book to her.

PREFACE

My introduction to Jennifer Higdon was through her choral music in 2008 when I served as Director of Choral Studies at Bowling Green State University (BGSU) in Ohio. BGSU is home to the annual New Music and Art Festival, which features esteemed contemporary composers and their new works, many of them premiers. Jennifer was invited to participate in this festival. Interestingly, Jennifer was a student at BGSU prior to my appointment.

After I later accepted a new position as Department Chair and Professor of Choral Music at Rhodes College in Memphis, Tennessee, a packet of Jennifer's small-form choral music arrived for my review. She had become an acclaimed composer, having won a Pulitzer Prize for her Violin Concerto in 2010. Her envelope of works went on a shelf for consideration for future concerts.

While Rhodes College did not offer a new music festival, it has for decades offered an esteemed and historical music lecture series entitled the Springfield Music Lecture Series. This series has brought internationally renowned and respected composers, theorists, and musicologists to campus annually for lectures and residencies. I contacted Jennifer in 2010 to see if she would consent to be our Springfield Lecturer for 2011–12, and she enthusiastically accepted.

Jennifer sent me a score and the yet-unpublished CD of the Atlanta Symphony Orchestra with Robert Spano conducting *The Singing Rooms*, a major work for violin, orchestra, and choir, with Jennifer Koh as the solo violinist. The piece resonated with me immediately, and we agreed I would conduct the work with the Rhodes College MasterSingers and the Memphis Symphony Orchestra for a performance during her weeklong residency.

The week of her visit was extraordinary, even life-changing for me. The lecture was inspiring and relevant, the symphony and chorus were electrified with her presence and her music, and the concert was enthusiastically received. Students found Jennifer to be extraordinarily approachable; they were thrilled and inspired to meet her and to hear her lecture and her music.

Jennifer informed me that *The Singing Rooms* had not yet been presented in Europe and that she would hold the European premier for me, if I would like. How does one say no to that? I had conducted a number of European choral festivals with orchestras, and so a performance was soon scheduled at La Madeleine in Paris for summer of 2014 through Music Celebrations International. Susanna Perry Gilmore was the violin soloist with a Parisian orchestra. The premier was attended by Jennifer, her business partner Cheryl Lawson, and Jeanne Minahan, the poet for *The Singing Rooms*. La Madeleine was packed, and the audience was immediately on their feet in a lengthy ovation for this extraordinary work.

In August of 2015, I attended one of the first performances of Jennifer's opera, *Cold Mountain*, in Santa Fe, New Mexico. It was an honor to sit with her and Cheryl for this performance, which was simply breathtaking. One chorus from that opera was subsequently extracted and became a stand-alone a cappella choral piece for male voices entitled *Our Beautiful Country*. My professional men's ensemble, BealeCanto, premiered this setting sometime later with Jennifer in the audience.

Following that experience, I asked if she would consider accepting a commission from Rhodes for a new work. Though she could not accept any new ones at that time, she said if I would consider a co-commission with another organization, something might work out. That led to a co-commission, ultimately based on several poems by Rumi, with the Washington Master Chorale. In April 2017, our regional premier of the subsequent piece, *Ruminations*, was presented along with *The Singing Rooms*, this time with Barrie Cooper, concertmaster for the Memphis Symphony Orchestra, as the solo violinist. Completing the program, the Rhodes choirs performed several of Higdon's shorter works, and BealeCanto premiered the new version of *Our Beautiful Country*. With Jennifer and Cheryl present, the concert received a lengthy standing ovation.

My wife, Elaine, purchased a book for me by Christina Reitz entitled *Jennifer Higdon: Composing in Color*, published in 2018. Elaine, who deserves credit for inspiring this project, told me that a companion book on Higdon's choral works was now needed. Jennifer and Cheryl agreed—but cautioned me that the aforementioned book took years in the making.

I am a conductor and educator; I live and breathe on the podium. Analysis is an essential part of what a conductor must do, and an analysis of music–text relationship is critical for conducting any choral work. I enjoy and even thrive on the thorough study of music. The process of writing, however, is a challenging one for me. But I had to agree with my wife: Jennifer's music was simply too important to allow it to live in obscurity. I felt compelled to take on what would become, over several years, an enormous but deeply meaningful project.

Her music is very special, unique, so worthy of dissemination, that I felt obligated to share my experiences. It has been, and continues to be, a special privilege to have performed much of her choral music, and personally knowing Jennifer, Cheryl, and Jeanne has enriched this experience for me.

As you read these pages, it is my hope that they might inspire you to listen to and appreciate Jennifer's compositions. I hope you will be drawn to attend concerts of her music, perhaps to study it, and to be grateful for inviting it into your life. Whatever inspires you to participate in Jennifer Higdon's music—as a performer, scholar, or audience member—it will have made this entire effort worthwhile.

FOREWORD

In my undergraduate years as a budding composer, I devoured with a ravenous appetite the music by leading women composers. I grew up performing, as a singer and pianist, music by many of the world's greatest composers, yet I cannot recall performing any particular piece by a woman. When I started college, the music library became a magical place to peruse score upon score of works by female composers. Jennifer Higdon's music, of course, was there. Her *blue cathedral* and *Concerto for Orchestra* introduced me to her intriguing compositional voice, and composers like her inspired me to pursue my dreams voraciously.

It is remarkable that her choral works have not been celebrated with the same fervor as her instrumental works. Sure, she is a masterful orchestrator with an incredible ear for color, but a deeper look into her choral pieces reveals her mastery of counterpoint and four-part chorale writing. Many of these pieces pay tribute to tradition with elegance and a fresh perspective.

Higdon's choral works prove her to be a truly American voice, adventurous and colorful, patriotic and thoughtful. Her *Southern Grace* set should be featured in choral literature classes and sung often by choirs of all sizes. *Alleluia* sparkles with exciting energy and would make an excellent concert opener. Parallels to today's pandemic and political division are easily found in *Our Beautiful Country*, an excerpt for TTBB choir from the opera *Cold Mountain*. My favorite discovery, her *O magnum mysterium*, shines in the most haunting and soulful way, a welcome and notable addition to the repertoire that showcases her keen sense of color and virtuosic instrumental writing.

Higdon is not just one of the top female composers of her generation, she is one of the top composers of her generation. I look forward to the day our gender becomes less of a distinguishing characteristic when our works are classified, catalogued, and taught. I am grateful that books like this are being written and for the continued growth I see in the musical community toward equity and diversity.

—Jocelyn Hagen
Composer / Performer / Publisher

CHAPTER ONE

INTRODUCTION

Mention the name Jennifer Higdon to most classical musicians and the response is near universal recognition for her instrumental compositions. In opera circles, she is hailed as a rising star due to the enormous success of *Cold Mountain* and anticipation for a commission she has underway. However, among choral musicians, there appears to be little to no awareness of her accomplishments as a composer of quality choral music.

Higdon's choral works are abundant, profound, varied, and highly acclaimed by those who know them. A full list is provided in the appendix. By her own admission, her instrumental works and opera have largely overshadowed the choral pieces. The book *Jennifer Higdon: Composing in Color* by Christina L. Reitz has greatly expanded the awareness of Higdon's instrumental output.[1] A similar resource has not yet been available for her choral music.

This book brings Higdon's choral works to light, exploring them with respect to their stylistic characteristics and their relationship between music and text. As an analytical piece, it reveals immediate and demonstrable connections between musical elements drawn directly from the text. A thorough analysis demonstrates that structure, melody, harmony, counterpoint, rhythm, meter, texture, and accompaniment are all intimately linked to the poetry. Often, several musical elements combine and conspire to bring out the meaning of the text.

To attempt to summarize any composer's theoretical tendencies is something of a slippery slope, as interpreting links between text and music is unavoidably threaded with a degree of subjectivity. But Higdon wholeheartedly embraces such deductions in analyses of her work.

As Higdon is not well known in the choral community, a brief introduction to her seems appropriate. She has become one of the most

---

[1]   Christina L. Reitz, *Jennifer Higdon: Composing in Color* (Jefferson, NC: McFarland and Company, Inc., 2018).

frequently performed living American composers.[2] She has received an abundance of commissions from prestigious musical organizations for orchestral works, operas, and choral compositions, large and small. Her work has attracted awards from the Guggenheim Foundation, the American Academy of Arts and Letters, the Koussevitzky Foundation, the Pew Fellowship in the Arts, and the National Endowment for the Arts. Most notably, her Viola Concerto won a Grammy for Best Contemporary Classical Composition in 2017, her Percussion Concerto won the same award in 2010, and in the same year she received the Pulitzer Prize in Music for her Violin Concerto, with the committee citing Higdon's work as "a deeply engaging piece that combines flowing lyricism with dazzling virtuosity."[3]

Higdon's choral works may have been overshadowed by those of other genres, but this is changing. Growing numbers of prestigious choral organizations are performing her works and making commissions. Their attention serves as evidence of the pieces' worthiness of critical scrutiny, bringing them to a level similar to her other genres.

This study offers representative stylistic characteristics of her choral pieces. It is tempting to refer to Higdon as a neo-Renaissance composer because of the close connection between her music and its text and since each line of a text seems to generate a new musical thought or region of construction. But that description, while appropriate in some ways, would fall far short of defining her overall compositional style. The compositional fabrics she weaves are diverse, complex, and contemporary.

She employs sophisticated forms based in traditional constructions. Though tonal, her works employ harmonic colors that are refreshing and distinctive. She frequently uses short motivic ideas that she expands and alters into thick contrapuntal fabrics. Complex rhythms and harmonies align with text structure, enunciation, and delivery. Her compositions, as communicated to this author by singers and audience members alike, tend to create "atmospheres" that at first blush give the impression of being somewhat transparent, seemingly accessible. Upon closer scrutiny, however, the compositional processes behind these effects are far more challenging than may have first appeared. Each work represents something

---

[2]   "Biography," *jenniferhigdon.com* (accessed January 16, 2021).

[3]   "*Violin Concerto*, by Jennifer Higdon (Lawdon Press)," Pulitzer Prize, 2010, https://www.pulitzer.org/winners/jennifer-higdon (accessed January 16, 2021).

of a musical mosaic; combinations of innovative musical elements are used to create form and to balance unity with variety.

Higdon's large-form choral works are accompanied by orchestra, and the small-form works are performed either a cappella or with chamber instruments. The secular pieces use English texts, and some of the sacred pieces use Latin. In the latter cases, such as in *O magnum mysterium* and *Sanctus*, Higdon ensures text comprehension by setting English translations alongside the Latin in the same piece, eliminating the language barrier for the singer and listener.

I have had the privilege of conducting many of Higdon's choral pieces with the composer present. I find them to be challenging, intriguing, highly effective, and inspirational in rehearsals and performance. Singers, instrumentalists, and audience members receive her work with tremendous enthusiasm and appreciation. I am grateful that Jennifer has given her strong support to this study.

An analysis of a relationship between text and music in any composer's works brings with it a degree of subjectivity and interpretation. The analyst must use his or her expertise to deduce the components of such connection with as keen an eye as he or she is able. To quote Keith Burris in his book on Robert Shaw, in doing such work, an author

> discovers how much he does not know, and can never know, about it. He discovers that he cannot, finally, "get to the bottom" of the subject's nature, though his job is to try. He knows he must be wary of broad claims and generalizations. ... So, [he] creates a portrait. He can only paint from his own perspective and his portrait cannot be other than subjective. For no two people see another in the same way.[4]

Burris is discussing a biography on Shaw, but his words resonate with this author as they relate to this discussion of Higdon and the analysis of her works. Higdon's compositional style does not lend itself to being succinctly summarized. It is the hope that this analysis will be of assistance in assessing and approaching her compositions and intrigue readers—inspiring them to delve further into her significant contributions to the choral repertoire.

Higdon continues to add to her work, which is already voluminous, creative, and deep in its offerings to this genre. Her future compositions are

---

[4]   Keith C. Burris, *The Life and Music of Robert Shaw* (Chicago: GIA Publications, 2013), xi–xii.

eagerly awaited. The music world will be well rewarded by growing awareness of her choral works and their more frequent presentation in concert.

CHAPTER TWO

THE SINGING ROOMS

The Singing Rooms
(2007) 37 minutes
In 7 movements
Full orchestra, SATB chorus, solo violin
2, 2 (2nd also Eng. hn.) 2, 2, 4, 3 (1st also picc. tpt.)
3, 1 hp., timp, 2 perc., strings
Poetry by Jeanne Minahan, secular/spiritual

Jennifer Higdon's ability to connect music with text is well illustrated in *The Singing Rooms*, a large-form work for choir, orchestra, and solo violinist. The work displays compositional traits that can be found in most of her choral compositions. Composed in 2007, its seven contiguous movements are set to six poems by Jeanne Minahan. As Higdon writes in the program notes on her website,

> When I was asked by the Philadelphia Orchestra to write a concerto for violin that would include a choral part, I immediately started searching through all sorts of poetry. The poetry would need to speak to me in order for me to be able to set it to music. ... To create the best form for the piece, I needed a group of poems that would not be too long (because I wanted to create different moods within this large work) and that would fit together thematically. I looked for a long time, through poetry from various countries and time periods. ... When I got some books of [Minahan's] poetry in my hands, I knew I had found what I was looking for—a series of poems that resonated with me and would provide different emotional settings, as if they were lessons in life arranged like different rooms within a house.[1]

Higdon adapted and edited the poems for her composition. In the score, Minahan's full poems are provided at the beginning of each movement.

As the piece is designed as one complete work, no movement can be extrapolated and performed on its own. Distinct musical elements characterize

---

[1] Jennifer Higdon, "Program Notes: *The Singing Rooms*," http://www.jenniferhigdon.com/pdf/program-notes/The-Singing-Rooms.pdf (accessed January 17, 2021).

each movement, and most are not directly connected to the others by poetic theme, except the first and last, which use the same text.

I. Three Windows: Two Versions of the Day (4′)

Three windows offer two versions of the day,
the first: cool and sweet, a blue cascade
of watered light,
the second: bright heat barely held back
by the venetian blind.

Inside, the blue falls across
the small kitchen (a breeze
at your back), and angles
into the living room where
the table and two chairs swim.

The couch, the desk, bookshelves,
the bed, they submit
each morning to the thin cloths of light
that drape, linger and slide
across them; its shape their shape.

Both are here, though you
cannot be:
that heat, that long shade of blue.

Higdon's dedication to painting the text in music is immediately evident: the orchestra produces an ethereal atmosphere for the mystery of the day ahead. The introduction begins with ambient percussion, including crotales mounted on timpani played while pedaling freely, and bowed vibraphone. Harmonics and other-worldly sounds fill the air, along with lilting, seemingly unmeasured counterpoint, together representing the mystery of time. The violin solo represents a soul traveling from room to room in search of the day's meaning.

This movement is characterized by secundal and quintal harmonies and Lydian mode, especially in the solo violin. In Higdon's choral works, Lydian is frequently associated with uplifting or ethereal passages, as in this introduction. The first notes of the chorus are stacked open fifths on the tuning notes of the violin, G–D–A–E (see Figure 2-1). These stacked fifths represent the spaciousness of the room, the expansiveness of the soul, and a link between the chorus and the violin.

Figure 2-1. Jennifer Higdon, *The Singing Rooms*, movement 1, mm. 7–12
Music Copyright © 2007 by Jennifer Higdon [ASCAP].
Poems Copyright by Jeanne Minahan.

"Three Windows: Two Versions of the Day" is constructed in seven short choral sections, the longest of which is eight measures. The longest choral sections are recitative-like passages that deliver a large amount of text quickly and transparently. The text is delivered without much melodic variance, and the rhythms align with natural scansion and syllabic inflection. This type of choral setting, called choral chant or choral recitative, is common in Higdon's works. Because the poetry is articulated without the interference of complex musical development, short segments of text are set to short motives of music.

Figure 2-2 shows an example of choral chant as well as parallel harmonic motion. Higdon often uses such planing to heighten the effect of an approaching cadence. In the ensuing section of choral chant as the chorus mentions the window's blinds, the blinds seem to close as the lines descend.

Figure 2-2. Jennifer Higdon, *The Singing Rooms*, movement 1, mm. 18–22
Music Copyright © 2007 by Jennifer Higdon [ASCAP].
Poems Copyright by Jeanne Minahan.

Higdon typically crafts choral lines that are narrow in range, somewhat in the lyric and expressive style of an art song, where rhythm, text, and modest melodic motion are bound to sensitive poetic expression. In Figure 2-3, the text "the couch, the desk, bookshelves" is set in such a fashion. The voices move in rhythms that articulate the natural inflection and rhythm of the poetry. The vocal harmony is in parallel thirds and incorporates the tones G–B–A–B (mm. 33–34), G–A–B (mm. 35–36), G–A–G (mm. 36–37), and F–E♭ (m. 38) before rising, still in parallel motion, to the prevailing tonality of B major in measure 40. These harmonies are freely used to provide a mystical reference to the effects of the morning light. The descending thirds seem to represent the "thin cloths of light that drape, linger and slide" mentioned in the poetry. Decorative instrumental commentary enhances the peacefulness of this sunlit room at the start of the day.

Figure 2-3. Jennifer Higdon, *The Singing Rooms*, movement 1, mm. 33–38
Music Copyright © 2007 by Jennifer Higdon [ASCAP].
Poems Copyright by Jeanne Minahan.

In Figure 2-4, the homophony gives way to interwoven lines. The tenor is particularly florid, though the bass serves this function more often in Higdon's choral works. The tenors, imitating the sopranos at a half-beat delay, hand off their movement to the basses, who resolve to the root of the harmony. The cascade through the voices characterizes the decaying light of day. One can almost see the light diminishing as the lines descend. The passage demonstrates one method of mood coloring in Higdon's writing.

Figure 2-4. Jennifer Higdon, *The Singing Rooms*, movement 1, mm. 44–46
Music Copyright © 2007 by Jennifer Higdon [ASCAP].
Poems Copyright by Jeanne Minahan.

Higdon often develops motives through rhythmic metamorphosis, using one rhythmic figure then adjusting it. When mixed meter or asymmetrical meter is used in choral portions, it brings the text either new meaning or heightened attention. One instance in which rhythm and meter enhance the text is in the treatment of the repeated word "blue" in Figure 2-5. The measures contract from 4/4 to 3/4 to 2/4 as the word is repeated in more compact and intensified statements. The word describes growing light coming through the windows as the day breaks.

Figure 2-5 also contains the movement's high point, which is in part accomplished through these altered rhythmic entrances and meters. The voices are in homophony, alternating between B major and F major, by roots of a tritone, and then between B major and G major, by roots of a third. The latter alternations are much more consonant and peaceful, but the tritone movement returns to end this section, perhaps emphasizing the volatility of life.

Figure 2-5. Jennifer Higdon, *The Singing Rooms*, movement 1, mm. 53–58
Music Copyright © 2007 by Jennifer Higdon [ASCAP].
Poems Copyright by Jeanne Minahan.

Choral passages in this movement are usually chordal and homophonic, but counterpoint occurs briefly during the final syllables of phrases, to color those moments. The seven choral passages deliver six sections of the poem, then repeat the poem's opening in the penultimate section of music before offering the seventh and final part of the poem. "Three Windows: Two Versions of the Day" concludes with a tense orchestral bridge that highlights the dramatic mystery of the windows.

II. Things Aren't Always (3′)

Not every newborn cries in hunger,
not every dog barks in alarm.
Musicians, on a whim,
break our hearts,
lovers take the blame.

When the orchestra pauses at the end of the previous movement, a single repeated note in the solo violin takes over, bringing the next room to explore. This pitch, E, is rhythmically varied and then expanded melodically, first to a half-step alternation with F, and then to other pitches. This introduction to movement two is lengthy, lasting seventy-nine measures.

The violin's E–F note alternation becomes the chorus's opening line (see Figure 2-6); this motive will be altered throughout the movement. The chorus sings again in planing choral chant, alternating between the chords of E minor and F major. The text is "Things Aren't Always," and, as events are not always predictable or consistent in life, likewise the alterations and adjustments around the note E. Higdon has explained that this poem means that "things in life are always changing, always moving... not at all what they seem."

Figure 2-6. Jennifer Higdon, *The Singing Rooms*, movement 2, mm. 80–81
Music Copyright © 2007 by Jennifer Higdon [ASCAP].
Poems Copyright by Jeanne Minahan.

The chorus never utters a complete, continuous phrase of text or melody; rather, they articulate splices of poetry set to short sections of music. The splices are then bridged by a few orchestral measures.

E minor is the dominant harmony in this movement, but subtle harmonic variations are coupled with text meaning. An example occurs in the phrase "Not every newborn cries in hunger," which begins alternating by thirds between the parallel triads E minor and G major. On the word "cries," the harmony changes to an F major triad (Figure 2-7)—here, the F major chord, broadened on a dotted-quarter note, paints a newborn's cries in real time. Attention is given to those cries by breaking from the harmonies that govern the movement.

Figure 2-7. Jennifer Higdon, *The Singing Rooms*, movement 2, mm. 85–87
Music Copyright © 2007 by Jennifer Higdon [ASCAP].
Poems Copyright by Jeanne Minahan.

While the first section ends in E minor on the word "hunger," the next section, set to the text "Not every dog barks," takes up F major. The solo violin's active line represents unsettled life amid constant changes. On the text "break our heart," the chorus breaks the rhythm; they match the idea of breaking in the text with a staccato note on beat one and a rest in beat four (Figure 2-8).

Figure 2-8. Jennifer Higdon, *The Singing Rooms*, movement 2, mm. 103–106
Music Copyright © 2007 by Jennifer Higdon [ASCAP].
Poems Copyright by Jeanne Minahan.

Concluding this movement is a protracted orchestral interlude. It develops the dominating half-step alternation motive. Modeling life's unpredictability, the orchestration escalates to a peak that ends suddenly and without resolution.

III. The Interpretation of Dreams (6′)

If I told you my dream
(the one on a boat);
if I told you how I read
your dream with a cello:
a new laugh
an old hush.

"The Interpretation of Dreams" has a different melodic character from the previous movement, appropriate to its different text. The poetry describes a dream sequence, which Higdon orchestrates with ethereal, other-worldly effects, achieved in part through a sudden shift in dynamics, tempo, and orchestration. Organic continuity between the movements is preserved as the previous movement's half-step motive is alluded to, overlaced with the violin in Lydian mode. The melody, akin to others in the work, begins with a short statement that expands and evolves into a longer statement. But in contrast with previous themes, this one is longer, more legato, and lyrical. It also uses wider intervals, ascending a major sixth; the larger melodic range helps to describe the elevation of a dream. In Higdon's words, the melody has "a gentle, boat-rocking sensation," which is achieved through alternations between high and low notes. See the first measures of Figure 2-9.

The short poem is stated three times, Higdon explains, "because it is the third poem in the set." The first four measures of the melody are built using a pentatonic scale, F–G–A–C–D. The melody, and this movement's theme, eventually expands to consist of seven different tones, the number of tones Higdon normally favors in her extended melodies. In the fifth measure, the melody changes to F Mixolydian for the text "a new laugh, an old hush"; the reference to newness, then, is set in a mode other than what was first used. The word "hush" ends the phrase on an open fifth, D–A: a "hush" is silence between utterances, and here the hush is delivered musically via the emptiness in that spacious interval. Lyricism, open fifths, and modal mixture typify this movement and bring out the dream aspect.

Consistent with Higdon's custom of starting with a short motive and then expanding it, the melody begins with unison sopranos, and then the altos, also in unison, are added. Finally, the male voices join in open fifths on the word "hush" and provide a sense of gravity to the word. Underneath, the lowest notes in the orchestration move in thirds, D–F–A♭, a pattern that Higdon relies on to convey moments of peace, rest, and consonance.

Figure 2-9. Jennifer Higdon, *The Singing Rooms*, movement 3, mm. 174–181
Music Copyright © 2007 by Jennifer Higdon [ASCAP].
Poems Copyright by Jeanne Minahan.

The second iteration of the poem repeats the theme with the sopranos and tenors in octaves (Figure 2-10). The vocal line is now in F Lydian; the foreign-sounding raised fourth scale degree, B♮, helps to characterize the dreamlike state. Further diffusing the harmonic predictability, Lydian is short-lived and E♭ enters in measure 179 (see Figure 2-9). Orchestral planing supports the dreamlike haze. Starting on beat 3 of measure 191, the harmony progresses as follows: B♭–A⁷–G–F–E♭–D♭–B–A♭. The progression is a stepwise descent until the second to last chord, which descends by a third—again, Higdon's preferred root movement for conveying serenity.

Figure 2-10. Jennifer Higdon, *The Singing Rooms*, movement 3, mm. 188–193
Music Copyright © 2007 by Jennifer Higdon [ASCAP].
Poems Copyright by Jeanne Minahan.

A lengthy orchestral development follows. Planing in the upper orchestra and a rocking motion in the solo violin and trumpet continue to convey the dreamlike state. The music builds to a high point, and, unusually, this movement's peak occurs during the orchestral interlude—during the wordless dream itself—rather than in a choral section. The interlude relaxes into the poem's third iteration.

This iteration has expanded into three-voice counterpoint that intertwines the sopranos, altos, and tenors. The main melody is set in alternating voices—a form of voice exchange—between the sopranos and tenors, as seen in Figure 2-11. This is another device that distinguishes

Higdon's work: she alternates words or syllables between voices, sometimes in a pointillistic fashion. In this case, subphrases of the melody are exchanged.

Figure 2-11. Jennifer Higdon, *The Singing Rooms*, movement 3, mm. 211–215
Music Copyright © 2007 by Jennifer Higdon [ASCAP].
Poems Copyright by Jeanne Minahan.

The cadence culminates in homophony in open fourths. An orchestral codetta follows using materials from the interlude and, like in the passage from movement two to movement three, a sudden shift of character begins the fourth movement, "Confession."

IV. Confession (6′40″)

Once I slept all night without dreaming
in the body of a small summer flower:
buttercup, yellow and damp,
circling me with warmth.

And I've taken tears from an earthen bowl,
clay pressed in a curve of bone:
a basin borne of rib and hip.
I drank and sang in sweet drunkenness.

Once I dressed in luminous dust
and set myself spinning in the Pleiades
just to be unseen among the seen.
I admit I've listened to the whistling of God,
kissed lips that were not mine or yours.

If I tell you these things now,
you must hold them in your palms
as I have seen you hold water:
cupped and uncontained.

Give me such forgiveness
as that:

liquid, poured out,
uncondemned
for being so clear.

As movement three portrays a dreamlike euphoria, movement four begins in another sleep state: "Once I slept all night without dreaming." But though poetic theme links the movements, their musical ideas are in contrast. Movement four commences in a similar manner to movement two, with an agitated violin solo that begins with two pitches, E and F. By way of rapid sixteenth-note patterns, the melody expands to include another note, then two more, and so on, culminating in a state of frenzy. The violin solo conveys the angst one might experience when anticipating one's own confession. Higdon explains that this idea was indeed her inspiration: "The fragility of handing over a confession to another is sometimes anxiety producing." Complex agitated rhythms and stacked seconds in the orchestration heighten and evolve, steadily intensifying until near the end of the thirty-seven-measure preamble. The mood of the music is ironic or paradoxical in relation to the opening phrase of text: the poem's speaker is clearly having a fitful sleep, without the repose of dreaming.

In anticipation of the first lines of the poem, "Once I slept all night without dreaming in the body of a small summer flower," the preamble thins and relaxes, as if to shift into a cocooned, dreamless sleep. The melody begins on F and gradually expands upward in pitch, mimicking the opening of a flower (Figure 2-12). In the descent of the phrase, creating the effect of the flower encircling the speaker, the voices fold downward in the same manner: "buttercup, yellow and damp, circling me with warmth." An orchestral interlude returns to driving sixteenth notes in the lower orchestration. The harmony is now in B♭ Lydian.

Figure 2-12. Jennifer Higdon, *The Singing Rooms*, movement 4, mm. 264–272
Music Copyright © 2007 by Jennifer Higdon [ASCAP].
Poems Copyright by Jeanne Minahan.

In the next phrase of poetry, "And I've taken tears from an earthen bowl," stacked seconds predominate, as they will throughout the movement. Higdon continues to use them in the next phrase, "a basin borne of rib and hip. I drank and sang in sweet drunkenness." Here, the chords descend in parallel motion, representing relaxation, while resolution to a Bb major triad represents the contentment found in "sweet drunkenness." Consonant resolution to a triad often follows the denser passages in Higdon's writing.

Sixteenth notes again occur in an extended orchestral interlude. The women's voices reenter on the text "Once I dressed in luminous dust." Descending seconds yield to added-note chords. The text "and set myself spinning in the Pleiades" is set to a six-note melody. Higdon explains that the Pleiades is

> an open star cluster in the constellation Taurus, which consists of several hundred stars, [but] only six visible to the human eye. I found this particular tidbit fascinating mostly because, before reading the definition, I had written a six-note figure for the violin that occurs repeatedly within this movement.

The chorus also has a six-note melody set in F Lydian, which then moves to Eb Lydian. Higdon uses modal exchange to create colorful cross-relations in the music that represent the delirium of spinning up to the constellation.

After the individual is set spinning, the choir sings breathless imitative utterances on the text "just to be unseen" (Figure 2-13). They arrive in homophony on "among the seen." This confession comes to peace on an open fifth, G and D. Elsewhere in this movement, a complete G major triad serves as the home chord that provides aural rest after dense counterpoint and harmonic dissonance. Here in the open fifth, the missing third might metaphorically stand for the things "to be unseen, among the seen."

Figure 2-13. Jennifer Higdon, *The Singing Rooms*, movement 4, mm. 301–306
Music Copyright © 2007 by Jennifer Higdon [ASCAP].
Poems Copyright by Jeanne Minahan.

Orchestral restlessness ensues with numerous seconds, complex rhythmic figures, and harmonic parallelism. Whereas in movement three the peak occurred in an orchestral passage, here the peak occurs in the chorus as they sing the text "I admit I've listened to the whistling of God" (Figure 2-14).

Figure 2-14. Jennifer Higdon, *The Singing Rooms*, movement 4, mm. 320–324
Music Copyright © 2007 by Jennifer Higdon [ASCAP].
Poems Copyright by Jeanne Minahan.

Often Higdon's compositions will build tension in polyphonic or contrapuntal textures and then gather into homophony at peak moments. This section of "Confession" demonstrates this. The chorus emerges in octaves out of the orchestral counterpoint. They move in parallel homophony, and then two measures later, they expand from octaves into chords that ascend to the word "God." Independent of the chorus, the orchestra descends in parallel motion from measure 322. Higdon normally writes lengthy peak sections, and in this case *ff* planing helps to achieve and maintain the climax. This section is climactic from measure 320, starting on the text "I admit I've listened to the whistling of God" (see above in Figure 2-14), and extends all the way to the cadence in measure 337, seen below in Figure 2-15.

D Lydian is hinted at for the text "If I tell you these things now, you must hold them in your palms." The texture then changes from homophony to counterpoint on the words "cupped and uncontained," and the imitative, descending counterpoint portrays the water that is "uncontained" and spilling out.

The angst associated with confession has not yet been relieved. The agitated violin solo and orchestration return. The chorus reemerges, pleading for grace: "Give me such forgiveness as that" (Figure 2-15). The ascending line strained with stacked seconds acts as a plea to God for peace. It is an uplifted prayer, unanswered: forgiveness is yet unreceived, and harmonic resolution yet unachieved. A moment of homophonic calm occurs on a G major triad in the alto and tenor on the text "liquid, poured out, uncondemned for being so clear." The harmonic resolution brings the sense of peace experienced after confession. The violin solo comes to the front again and dances in slurred bariolage.

Figure 2-15. Jennifer Higdon, *The Singing Rooms*, movement 4, mm. 354–363
Music Copyright © 2007 by Jennifer Higdon [ASCAP].
Poems Copyright by Jeanne Minahan.

The violin begins "Confession" with a motive conveying the angst of confession. It is used again in the interlude and here at the end of the movement. Its recurrence maintains the unsettled energy that defines the poem. At the very end, the violin line slows and relaxes, though it contains the same minor seconds with which it began. Minor seconds connected movement three to movement four and they bridge into movement five as well. In Figure 2-16, the violin line at the beginning of movement four and at its end is represented in the upper notes of the score reduction.

Figure 2-16. Jennifer Higdon, *The Singing Rooms*,
movement 4, mm. 223–225 and mm. 398–402
Music Copyright © 2007 by Jennifer Higdon [ASCAP].

V. History Lesson (3′)

How brief the pause
  between despair and comfort
                        How eternal.
How small the space
  between the window and frame.
                        How cold the wind.
[Teach me which of the stars have shifted.
Tell me where error crept in. Show me
the overlooked weed, infection, accounting mistake.
Adjust my glasses, hearing, fingertips.
Point me to the abandoned faith.]
When the day dims
  light the largest fire, cliff high.
And when they tell the story
  of these sad times
                        Remember
we lit that fire
  to spare the other ships
  these treacherous rocks…

"History Lesson" lasts but three minutes. As Higdon has explained, its brevity, as well as the brevity of the musical phrases within it, is calculated. She composed in this format as "an intentional decision to reflect on how we seem to remember the lessons of history for such short moments of time." Historical memory is indeed short. Disinclined to learn lessons from the past, we are doomed to repeat it.

From the movement's start, a field drum beats a halting rhythm that conveys trepidation (Figure 2-17). Like in previous movements, an E–F half step is rhythmically varied, this time in the percussion. The pitch E is subsequently intoned in repeated one-note entrances in the tenors. These entrances are staggered and defy predictability—the rests between them vary in length, as does the unpredictable progression of history. The tenors repeat one word, "How," again expressing uncertainty. Eighteen measures of such iterations occur before more words are sung. Meanwhile the strings play motives distinct from the singers'; the unsettling, cross-rhythmic underlay enhances the uncertainty in the text.

Figure 2-17. Jennifer Higdon, *The Singing Rooms*, movement 5, mm. 403–408
Music Copyright © 2007 by Jennifer Higdon [ASCAP].
Poems Copyright by Jeanne Minahan.

In the complete opening line of the poem, "How brief the pause between despair and comfort," brief pauses are appropriately created through intermittent rests (Figure 2-18). The melody is composed only of D and E, the narrow interval of a major second. Higdon changes to a comparatively lyric texture for the next text, "how eternal," where a four-part male chorus sings E minor to F major triads. The fragmented D and E melody returns for the phrase "How small the space between window and frame." The alternating notes a second apart, broken with rhythmic interruptions, musically illustrate the two objects, a window and a frame, with a narrow space between. For the text, "How cold the wind," the altos are added to the voicing, the rhythms are augmented, and parallel chords are used to characterize the bitter, blowing chill.

Figure 2-18. Jennifer Higdon, *The Singing Rooms*, movement 5, mm. 421–431
Music Copyright © 2007 by Jennifer Higdon [ASCAP].
Poems Copyright by Jeanne Minahan.

One of the more riveting moments of Higdon's writing occurs on the text "Teach me which of the stars have shifted." To express the physical shifting of the stars, the chorus sings B major and C major chords in alternating motion, as seen in Figure 2-19. This passage demonstrates just how detailed her work is in regard to delivering the text in a powerful, descriptive manner. It is a stunning moment in both the music and poetry, and the first of the two peaks in the movement.

Figure 2-19. Jennifer Higdon, *The Singing Rooms*, movement 5, mm. 434–435
Music Copyright © 2007 by Jennifer Higdon [ASCAP].
Poems Copyright by Jeanne Minahan.

Choral chant is used to deliver the phrase "Show me the overlooked weed, infection, accounting mistake. Adjust my glasses, hearing, fingertips" (Figure 2-20). The words are rapidly articulated in parallel motion and in relatively static harmony.

Figure 2-20. Jennifer Higdon, *The Singing Rooms*, movement 5, mm. 442–444
Music Copyright © 2007 by Jennifer Higdon [ASCAP].
Poems Copyright by Jeanne Minahan.

Higdon then moves to a broader, augmented homophony on the second, more emphatic peak with the text "Point me to the abandoned faith." After another orchestral reflection, the altos bring back the tenors' opening motive; they sing not "How" but "When." They intone the word on one pitch, repeating it over two measures (Figure 2-21). This is frustrated urging, to ask when history's lessons will be learned. In a brilliant use of voicing, it is the women that raise the question of when warfare might terminate, as the men are the ones historically more likely to wage war.

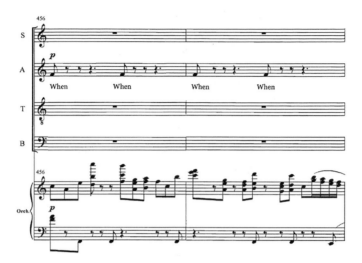

Figure 2-21. Jennifer Higdon, *The Singing Rooms*, movement 5, mm. 456–457
Music Copyright © 2007 by Jennifer Higdon [ASCAP].
Poems Copyright by Jeanne Minahan.

On the text "When the day dims, light the largest fire, cliff high," in measures 459–467, the female voices sing an arched contour, graphically portraying the rising flames of a warning fire. The flames' intensity is conveyed in the added seconds (Figure 2-22). The female voices continue, "And when they tell the story of these sad times," before the altos and tenors plead in unison for us to "Remember."

Figure 2-22. Jennifer Higdon, *The Singing Rooms*, movement 5, mm. 459–470
Music Copyright © 2007 by Jennifer Higdon [ASCAP].
Poems Copyright by Jeanne Minahan.

The first section of this piece was defined by the word "how"; the second, "when." In the third and final section, listeners are urged to learn from history so that they might spare themselves and others similar calamities. As the choir sings "we lit that fire to spare the other ships," they describe lighting a warning fire so that others may learn from the errors of history. The altos and tenors return in unison to sing "to spare the other ships these treacherous rocks"; this occurs in the same pattern as the two-note phrase in irregular, broken rhythms that was sung on the poem's first full line. The broken and active rhythms imply that the history lesson is ongoing, as yet unlearned and unstable. Human nature acts outside of its own interests. The music returns as in the opening, as history will likely repeat itself regardless of warnings. The orchestration augments, relaxes downward, and concludes with a tritone in the melody—which is fairly unusual for Higdon. The unstable interval heard here stands for the unlearned lesson.

The end of the fifth movement and the beginning of the sixth (see Figure 2-23) are nearly a mirror image of each other. These are the most self-reflective, internally gazing moments of the work.

Figure 2-23. Jennifer Higdon, *The Singing Rooms*, movement 5, mm. 485–490
Music Copyright © 2007 by Jennifer Higdon [ASCAP].
Poems Copyright by Jeanne Minahan.

VI. A Word with God (9′)

An áit a bhfuil do chroí is ann a thabhaifas do chosa thú.
"Your feet will bring you to where your heart is." (Irish Proverb)

And, finally we ask ourselves,
where did we spend our days, whose voice
turned our heads, hushed, thrilled,
entered, lingered, left us?

(Standing on a far shore,
uncertain of the hour or day
in a quiet not quiet.)

I walk towards you, I walk away;
my feet pull me back.
Wild One, your magnetic love
draws me (polar eclipse and warm),
you are the paradox towards which
I tend, you are the ache,
I don't need to speak,
you are the name of all names.

This is the work's most extensive movement, and it begins with one of the quietest, most transparent moments: a ballet-like, free-flowing conversation between the solo violin and English horn. This slow duet lasting twenty-four measures represents an intimate, personal conversation between an individual and God. As Higdon has expressed,

> For a composer, it is intimidating to think of how one sets into music such a thing as speaking to God … But I love the idea of starting it as an intimate conversation, so I wrote a duet between the English horn and solo violin, which eventually evolves into a series of emotions and conversations, adding voices and varying degrees of urgency.

It is significant that Higdon speaks of the construction of this movement entirely with respect to the poetry—not in terms of her musical idioms or ideas but in terms of the text and characters.

The soulful duet introduces the return of the chorus and orchestra and the final poem. The sopranos begin and are subsequently imitated by the altos, tenors, and basses: "And, finally, we ask ourselves, where did we spend our days" (Figure 2-24). It is a profound question that we indeed ponder when faced with whom, or what, we perceive God to be.

Descending voice assignments are used throughout this work to bring attention to the words upon which they are sung. In this case, the singers are soul-searching; their breathing, sighing motive ascends and then descends. The contours imply resignation and acceptance, a coming to the end of a futile striving for wisdom, knowledge, grace, and internal peace; perhaps we are near the end of human understanding.

Figure 2-24. Jennifer Higdon, *The Singing Rooms*, movement 6, mm. 511–512
Music Copyright © 2007 by Jennifer Higdon [ASCAP].
Poems Copyright by Jeanne Minahan.

The next section is longer and more elaborate than any preceding passage, and it brings the climax for the entire forty-minute work. It begins at the statement "Standing on a far shore, uncertain of the hour or day" (Figure 2-25). For the first and only time in the piece, multiple polychords occur. The women articulate a G^7 chord against D minor^9 in the male voices; they move to F major^7 against B♭ major, then D^7 against G major. The polychords represent the separation of someone standing on a far shore, removed from home, family, familiarity, safety, and security. The separation is enhanced by the gender-specific voicing.

Figure 2-25. Jennifer Higdon, *The Singing Rooms*, movement 6, mm. 523–528
Music Copyright © 2007 by Jennifer Higdon [ASCAP].
Poems Copyright by Jeanne Minahan.

Next appears an imbalanced rhythmic device similar to the one found on the words "How" and "When" in "History Lesson." The text, now repeated in offbeat, staggered fragments, is "In a quiet not quiet" (Figure 2-26). The effect is restlessness, perhaps in the search for ever-elusive peace. Higdon sets these fragments on parallel chords in the three upper voices.

Figure 2-26. Jennifer Higdon, *The Singing Rooms*, movement 6, mm. 529–534
Music Copyright © 2007 by Jennifer Higdon [ASCAP].
Poems Copyright by Jeanne Minahan.

A lyric section ensues. In a quasi-recitative in the bass voices in measures 534–538, "I walk, I walk, I walk, I walk toward you," the basses seem to walk forward in their independent, rhythmic monotone (Figure 2-27). They are joined by the other voices once again in polychords, which are by now a characterizing device for this movement, here laced with added seconds and dissonance. The act of walking toward God is portrayed as fraught, as the music contains the most thorny, dissonant choral writing in the composition. Rogue contrapuntal lines, which represent conflicting desires, occur in the altos and basses for a repeat of the text "I walk away." Ambivalence is again represented at the next line, "My feet pull me back," also set to polychords. The choir builds in parallel chords, and the poetry is repeated for an arrival on the home G major triad. The orchestration, meanwhile, has underscored the escalating internal tension. The violin solo, soaring and dancing during this time, represents being pulled in the direction of God.

Figure 2-27. Jennifer Higdon, *The Singing Rooms*, movement 6, mm. 534–548
Music Copyright © 2007 by Jennifer Higdon [ASCAP].
Poems Copyright by Jeanne Minahan.

The music is almost unraveling at this point. Amidst dense and active orchestration, the chorus emerges on the text

Wild One, your magnetic love draws me (polar eclipse and warm), you are the paradox towards which I tend, you are the ache, I don't need to speak, you are the name of all names.

D Lydian brings an exhilarating uplift. Figure 2-28 shows parallel ascending chords in reference to God, set in choral homophony. Measures 578–580 close the peak, as the voices descend and land on a D major triad. Their downward evolution represents the solemnity of God, the "name of all names." Higdon again puts the male voices in counterpoint against the female voices. This is a weighty piece of music and text, where orchestra and chorus are gathered in full force.

Figure 2-28. Jennifer Higdon, *The Singing Rooms*, movement 6, mm. 570–580
Music Copyright © 2007 by Jennifer Higdon [ASCAP].
Poems Copyright by Jeanne Minahan.

A celebrative orchestral interlude ensues, and the violin solo emerges from the fray in measure 582 (Figure 2-29). Its bariolage first represents the overwhelmingness of this moment; then its descending lyric line expresses a more personal sense of resolve (Figure 2-30).

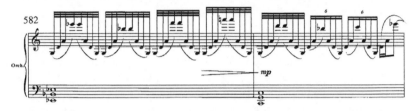

Figure 2-29. Jennifer Higdon, *The Singing Rooms*, movement 6, mm. 582–583
Music Copyright © 2007 by Jennifer Higdon [ASCAP].

Figure 2-30. Jennifer Higdon, *The Singing Rooms*, movement 6, mm. 589–291
Music Copyright © 2007 by Jennifer Higdon [ASCAP].

This brings a polytonal closing section in parallel chords for the orchestra. In measures 590–591 (see Figure 2-31), the altos sing a descending melody, C, B♭, A, G, F, adapted from the violin's line seen above in Figure 2-30. The melody is set to the Irish proverb, "Your feet will bring you to where your heart is." The altos sing the proverb three times. The last time, the other voices, female then male, join. The phrase culminates peacefully in the last measure with a G major home triad on "where the heart is."

Figure 2-31. Jennifer Higdon, *The Singing Rooms*, movement 6, mm. 593–604
Music Copyright © 2007 by Jennifer Higdon [ASCAP].
Poems Copyright by Jeanne Minahan.

VII. Three Windows: Two Versions of the Day (4′37″)

Before the last movement, there is a pause. It is the only time prolonged silence occurs in the work.

When the chorus reenters with the second version of "Three Windows: Two Versions of the Day," they sing on the open fifths of the violin tuning once more. In the opening movement, they were joined by the solo violin; here they are a cappella, an important difference, as the music is now completely self-reflective. This version contrasts rhythmically and metrically from the first movement; the meter is now 4/4 instead of 3/4, and quarter notes are used rather than the original eighth notes. Some things immediately recall the work's opening: the exact text, of course. But as there are two versions of the day, now there are two versions of the music. In Higdon's words,

> The second setting of this poem presents the second version of the day: a view at the close in the day of life … a return to the original poem, but with wisdom gained and all seen in a new light.

Figure 2-32 shows descending counterpoint in the alto and bass that is different from what occurred in the first movement. Our perception of the day has changed now that we have reached its close.

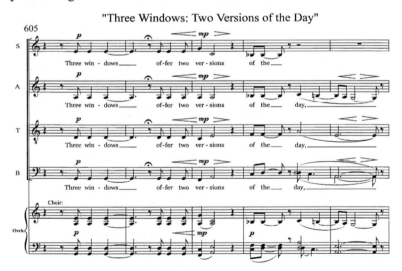

Figure 2-32. Jennifer Higdon, *The Singing Rooms*, movement 7, mm. 605–609
Music Copyright © 2007 by Jennifer Higdon [ASCAP].
Poems Copyright by Jeanne Minahan.

More variation occurs throughout the movement. The tenors and altos enter into a contrapuntal dance at the text "Inside, the blue falls across the small kitchen," whereas in the first section, these two were in unison. "And angles into the living room" is now set for sopranos and tenors, instead of a unison tenor line. The musical textures and additional voices create an impression of growth, change, and maturation. The understated peak of this movement, "Both are here, though you cannot be," is homophonic, without imitation as in the first movement (Figure 2-33). The homophony signals that we enter the room together in spirit.

Figure 2-33. Jennifer Higdon, *The Singing Rooms*, movement 7, mm. 636–639
Music Copyright © 2007 by Jennifer Higdon [ASCAP].
Poems Copyright by Jeanne Minahan.

This multi-sectional composition concludes much as it began. Simple choral lines begin the final section, starting in measure 642 (Figure 2-34), in transparent voice layering, with a hint of voice exchange between the tenors and altos on the final line, "that heat, that long shade of blue." The reader will recall that the word "blue" appeared early in this work at a climatic point, representing light and life. Now it is the final word, at the final moment of the day. It is set quietly in unison tones, reflective and unifying.

After all of the complexities of this substantial work, a single line of text is extended through voice exchange, melting into the orchestral fabric. The voices evaporate into the serene tones of violin harmonics and solo crotales on the timpani, as the light fades and the day draws to a close. While the chorus delivers the poetry, it is the orchestra that has the first and last say. These orchestral bookends allow time to anticipate and then reflect upon Minahan's poetry.

Figure 2-34. Jennifer Higdon, *The Singing Rooms*, movement 7, mm. 642–656
Music Copyright © 2007 by Jennifer Higdon [ASCAP].
Poems Copyright by Jeanne Minahan.

Summary of *The Singing Rooms*

The Singing Rooms is a powerful and profound collaboration of music and poetry. It represents spiritual perceptions throughout a given day, as a metaphor for the progression through life. The intricacies of the composition reveal aspects of the mystery of life on earth and, perhaps, beyond. Higdon judiciously selected Minahan's poetry for this transcendent journey.

The music is at times amorphous, haunting, and mysterious. Other times, it is dramatic, disturbing, demanding, and powerful. Often it is a combination of these elements. Clarity of the text is essential to the overall impact of the work and is supported by a coordination and convergence of musical elements. This musical-poetic drama, scored for large choral and orchestral forces with a virtuosic violin solo, is delivered in an exceedingly dramatic yet intimately soulful way.

After experiencing this composition and Higdon's choral works collectively, a question emerges: what is it that gives them such profound impact? What is it that makes them speak, what makes them new, unusual, and effective? The answer lies somewhere in the intricate web of techniques that Higdon coordinates to interpret and reveal aspects of the poems.

The poetry speaks profoundly by itself, yet Higdon's representation of the poems through her music communicates something of greater depth. Both performers and audience identify with and are subsequently moved by the piece's meaning. Taken individually, no single musical technique focused on text-painting would make Higdon's choral music necessarily special. It is when the techniques are perceived in consort with one another that their impact is experienced. Melody, harmony, rhythm, meter, structure, texture, counterpoint, development, and instrumentation collectively underscore and highlight the poetry. It is here that the magic that is Jennifer Higdon is felt and appreciated.

CHAPTER THREE

ON THE DEATH OF THE RIGHTEOUS

On the Death of the Righteous
(2009) 12 1/2 minutes
Full orchestra, SATB chorus
3 (3rd also picc.), 2, 2, 4, 4, 5, 3 picc. trpt., 3, 3, 1, timp., 1 perc., strings
Text by John Donne, sacred

*They shall awake and they shall say, Surely the Lord is in this place, and this is no
other but the house of God, and the gate of heaven.*

> *And into that gate they shall enter,*
> *And in that house they shall dwell,*
> *Where there shall be no Cloud nor Sun,*
> *No darkness nor dazzling,*
> *But one equal light,*
> *No noise nor silence,*
> *But one equal music,*
> *No fears nor hopes,*
> *But one equal possession,*
> *No foes nor friends,*
> *But one equal communion,*
> *No ends nor beginnings,*
> *But one equal eternity.*
> *Keep us Lord so awake in the duties of our callings, that we may thus sleep
> in Thy Peace, and wake in Thy Glory ...*

John Donne, *Sermons*, VIII, 191

Jennifer Higdon's *On the Death of the Righteous* is a large-form work
in one movement scored for full orchestra and large chorus. The
Mendelssohn Club in Philadelphia commissioned the piece to be paired in
performance with Giuseppe Verdi's *Requiem*. Accordingly, Higdon scored
On the Death of the Righteous with similar orchestration, including four
offstage trumpets in addition to the four onstage. The piece is through-
composed to match the form of the text.

The text, which Higdon selected in collaboration with the commissioning
agent, is from a sermon written in 1627 by the Anglican cleric John Donne.

In her program notes, Higdon explains what drew her to the text:

> Finding a text to be a part of a piece that would share a program with Verdi's *Requiem* was an interesting challenge … I needed something that would respect a requiem's definition, which is to be a mass for the dead. Coming upon Mr. Donne's sermons, I discovered a particular text that describes the nonjudgmental quality of a death of one who is righteous … this seemed an appropriate emotional angle to precede a requiem.[1]

Although Higdon's text selections are often secular and Donne's text is sacred, it shares characteristics with texts in her other works. Her chosen texts blend the sacred with the secular and emphasize the social, the humane, the spiritual, and the mystery of life and what might lie beyond.

Higdon spends considerable time with a chosen text before she begins composing. As she writes,

> I try to sit with the text and let it tell me how the setting should go. When I've gone in with a preconceived idea of how a work should be written, I've often had to scratch entire sections because they just did not work. It is always a surprise but I have found that, in the end, my original idea would not have been nearly as good. For me, it is important to try to listen to the text.[2]

Opening

Higdon establishes the tone for her choral compositions through an introductory section that creates an ambience or mood before the main thematic ideas begin. In works with orchestra, these introductions are instrumental. *On the Death of the Righteous* begins with two measures of a thin, ethereal woodwind quintet and ambient percussion. These instruments provide an austere backdrop for the entrance of chant-like rhythms from the choir (Figure 3-1). As a post-tonal composer, Higdon does not work in predetermined key schemes or established tonal centers; yet her music is accessible, friendly to the ear, and expressive. Higdon has explained that

> When I am doing sketches … something will occur to me and I try to find it on the piano. I never pay attention to the key. People tell me, "Oh, this is in such-and-such key," I have to go back and look at the score. I don't know. At no point when I am composing, do I ever think, "This is in the

---

[1]   Jennifer Higdon, "Program Notes: *On the Death of the Righteous*," http://www.jenniferhigdon.com/pdf/program-notes/On-the-Death-of-the-Righteous.pdf, retrieved September 14, 2015.

[2]   Jennifer Higdon, email to the author, March 31, 2020.

key of …"[3]

The tenors enter in measure 3 intoning the words "On the Death of the Righteous" on the pitch A. When they eventually change pitch several measures later, they move in mostly stepwise motion. Their line is chant-like, evoking the centuries-old tradition of church music and the period in which Donne lived. The drone-like dirge characterizes the mystery of someone who is in the transitory state of dying.

The orchestration is at first minimal but builds and intensifies through rhythmic diminution—becoming progressively faster under the tenors' steady chant. Other voices subsequently join. Clarity is maintained through contrapuntal techniques such as intervallic expansion, imitation, augmentation, and diminution. As the orchestra rarely doubles the chorus, the text remains clear.

Figure 3-1. Jennifer Higdon, *On the Death of the Righteous*, mm. 1–9
Music Copyright © 2008 by Jennifer Higdon [ASCAP].
Text by John Donne.

---

[3]   Christina L. Reitz, *Composing in Color* (Jefferson: McFarland & Company, Inc., 2018), 85.

In measure 13, the tenors begin repeating the text "They shall awake and they shall say." The bass section joins in stacked seconds, and then the altos in intervallic seconds. This harmonic widening and addition of voices portrays the persons who are being awakened. Full SATB voicing is achieved on the phrase "Surely the Lord is in this place" (Figure 3-2), as the sopranos join in stacked seconds and the harmony becomes even more dense. Through their abundance, stacked seconds emerge as one of the work's main characteristics. Their dissonance and harmonic thickness may represent death, but death with transfiguration: mystery, awe, reverence, and fear of the unknown remain the predominant impressions that Higdon conveys throughout the piece.

Another consistent Higdon trait is to bring up a given mode but not strictly stay within it. Such is the case here: references to B♭ Lydian are found through this opening section with the intermittent presence of E♮s, as in the soprano line in measure 19 on the word "surely."

Polychords are a tool that Higdon uses to unsettle particular words. In measure 21 on the word "place," she combines an F major triad with a G major triad. This polychord, which is voiced with stacked seconds, inspires a sense of confusion, excitement, and even anxiety at the Lord's presence. Such chords might arguably be analyzed as thirteenth or fifteenth chords, but due to their harmonic instability, they sound like polychords. Higdon often employs harmonies that obscure the tonality. Her harmonic techniques can include color chords, such as polytonal allusions (or highly involved chord extensions), as well as quartal, quintal, and secundal or added-tone harmonies. Higdon connects the polytonal allusions to specific poetic moments. They appear in peak moments of stress, and often in cadences when she wishes to emphasize a given word.

Figure 3-2. Jennifer Higdon, *On the Death of the Righteous*, mm. 17–21
Music Copyright © 2008 by Jennifer Higdon [ΛSCΛP].
Text by John Donne.

Over measures 24–28 (Figure 3-3), the melody descends on the text "and the gate of heaven," though one might expect the word "heaven" to naturally ascend. This descent conveys serenity and portrays the movement of heaven's gates as they open to welcome the passing individual. The secundal harmonies thin and give way to a pure triad. The harmony resolves from an Ab triad to an Eb major seventh and then a Db major triad, indicating peaceful arrival in heaven.

Figure 3-3. Jennifer Higdon, *On the Death of the Righteous*, mm. 24–28
Music Copyright © 2008 by Jennifer Higdon [ASCAP].
Text by John Donne.

"And into that gate they shall enter"

The next small section incorporates a longer text: "And into that gate they shall enter, and in that house they shall dwell, where there shall be no cloud nor sun, no darkness, no dazzling but one equal light, No noise nor silence." The text is delivered in gentle homorhythm. The phrase "And into that gate they shall enter" in measures 28–30 (Figure 3-4) begins with chant-like intonation on an Ab in the soprano, in reference to the work's opening. The upper three voices sing in consonant and mostly parallel motion. Johann Sebastian Bach used threes as a religious reference in his music, but Higdon does not typically employ that symbol. About the appearance of instruments grouped in threes in her *Concerto for Orchestra*, Higdon stated, "The number three doesn't have to do with anything [such as reference to the Holy Trinity] ... it was a coincidence just because that was the size of the orchestra."[4]

Consonant triads from the key of Db major form the primary harmony. Color chords emphasize "gate" in measure 29 and "house" in measure 31; quartal chords ground "they shall" in measure 29 and "cloud" in measures 33–34. Over measures 34–36, parallel seconds appear on every syllable of the text "no dazzling but one equal light." The orchestration of this section is beautiful and austere, the consonant triads supported by gentle sixteenth-note triplet and eighth-note rhythms for trumpets and percussion. The effect is evocative of a ghostly march of saints. It is this kind of scoring that reveals Higdon's ability to subtly orchestrate a mood and animate a text. The text "no noise nor silence" in measures 37–40 is a cappella.

---

4   Christina L. Reitz, *Composing in Color* (Jefferson: McFarland & Company, Inc., 2018), 57.

Figure 3-4. Jennifer Higdon, *On the Death of the Righteous*, mm. 28–40
Music Copyright © 2008 by Jennifer Higdon [ASCAP].
Text by John Donne.

"But one equal music"

Following a brief pause, the counterpoint in measures 41–47 (Figure 3-5a) stands in immediate contrast to the preceding homorhythmic, chant-like section. The words "But one equal music" are repeated in imitative counterpoint, motivic fragmentation with rhythmic diminution, and melodic sequencing into stretto.

Figure 3-5a. Jennifer Higdon, *On the Death of the Righteous*, mm. 41–47
Music Copyright © 2008 by Jennifer Higdon [ASCAP].
Text by John Donne.

The phrase ascends and builds rapidly to a peak in measures 47–52. The concept of "one equal music" is emphasized through independent voicing, as if to illustrate that all voices are equal.

Higdon's music often employs chordal parallelism, as seen in measure 51 in the descending major triads of A, G, F, E, and D. Such parallel, triadic motion often emphasizes poetic endings at climactic cadential points (Figure 3-5b).

Figure 3-5b. Jennifer Higdon, *On the Death of the Righteous*, mm. 47–52
Music Copyright © 2008 by Jennifer Higdon [ASCAP].
Text by John Donne.

"No foes, nor friends"

Special importance is given to the text "No foes, nor friends, but one equal communion, No ends nor beginnings, But one equal eternity." As seen in Figure 3-6a, this section begins in an intoning, chant-like style, much like at the piece's start, but it builds to a peak in measures 60–63 (Figure 3-6b).

Figure 3-6a. Jennifer Higdon, *On the Death of the Righteous*, mm. 53–58
Music Copyright © 2008 by Jennifer Higdon [ASCAP].
Text by John Donne.

In measures 60–61, offbeat accentuations in the strings with rapid, accented embellishments from the woodwinds enhance the transient, unstable sense found in the words "no ends nor beginnings." The underlying animated brass harmonically reinforces the choir and gives energy to the text without interfering with its apprehension.

Figure 3-6b. Jennifer Higdon, *On the Death of the Righteous*, mm. 59–63
Music Copyright © 2008 by Jennifer Higdon [ASCAP].
Text by John Donne.

"Keep us Lord so awake"

In measure 64 (Figure 3-7) the choir pleads in a high tessitura, "Keep us Lord so awake in the duties of our callings." The voices move in parallel homophonic motion in a sort of arhythmic march. The harmony leaves the A major grounding and commences on a G major triad, evolving immediately into a section of choral planing that provides heightened drama. Except when A major grounds key moments, the harmony is unstable. For instance, D major and D minor alternate on the text "that we may thus sleep," creating the impression of drifting off to sleep. The harmony then shifts from D minor to B♭ major, a root movement by a third, on the word "peace," suggesting the sublime nature of spiritual sleep.

In Higdon's compositional style, unanticipated harmonic and melodic elements are used to highlight the meaning of the text and delivery. In one such phrase, "and wake in Thy Glory!" (measure 69), Higdon shifts from A major to A minor on the two syllables of the word "Glory," creating unexpected instability and an impression of wonder. When this text is repeated in measures 175–178, it culminates while remaining in A major, which by that point has become a gravitational home tone in this work. Cadencing on this chord provides a sense of stability and consonance. This cadential behavior, in which certain words become associated with certain harmonic ideas, is one way in which Higdon colors the text with musical devices that impact how an audience is affected by Donne's words.

Figure 3-7. Jennifer Higdon, *On the Death of the Righteous*, mm. 64–69
Music Copyright © 2008 by Jennifer Higdon [ASCAP].
Text by John Donne.

The choir to this point has been building slowly and insistently, with offbeats in the orchestra. A volatile twelve-measure orchestral interlude follows (Figure 3-8). The passage is marked by sixteenth notes, thirty-second notes, and sixteenth-note triplets in rippling scalar passages, polytonal allusions, and tritones. The passage is grounded in or around the tonality of B major for the partial cadences in measures 71, 73, 77, and in the ultimate orchestral resolution in measure 80, where B major in the strings and chimes is set over a destabilizing A pedal.

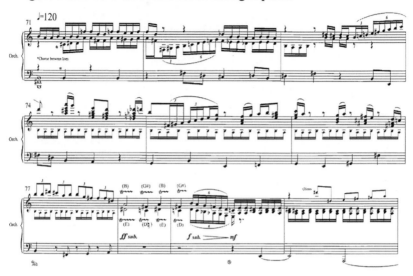

Figure 3-8. Jennifer Higdon, *On the Death of the Righteous*, mm. 71–80
Music Copyright © 2008 by Jennifer Higdon [ASCAP].

Higdon's scoring of this interlude is complementary to the vocal writing. Though the melodies are different, the orchestra's rhythmic vitality, counterpoint, and use of scalar passages and tritones correspond with the choir's passages.

Over measures 88–94, seen in Figure 3-9, for example, running sixteenth notes in the orchestra create a sense of restlessness under the choir. The text "house of God" in measures 90–91 is heightened as the orchestra sequences from G Lydian into A Lydian, with the raised fourth and fifth scale degrees of C♯ and D♯. On the word "God" in measure 91, Higdon superimposes A major and B major, again using a dissonant polychord to evoke intense awe. Splices of text correspond with splices of melody; as words are added, so are longer melodies, building to a peak over measures 88–95. After a stretch of four-part secundal writing, the voices arrive together on "Heaven."

The harmony over this section evolves from G Lydian in measure 87, to A Lydian by measure 90 beat 3, to a culmination in measure 94 on the root B against C♯ minor. This results in an ascending harmonic root motion of G–A–B to the word "Heaven," a moment painting spiritual, harmonic, and melodic ascension.

Figure 3-9. Jennifer Higdon, *On the Death of the Righteous*, mm. 88–95
Music Copyright © 2008 by Jennifer Higdon [ASCAP].
Text by John Donne.

"And into that gate they shall enter"

Gradually the driving rhythmic figures quiet, and the orchestration thins out in preparation for the reentry of the choir in measure 104 (Figure 3-10). This is characteristic of Higdon's developmental technique: she achieves dramatic impact through contrast, as high-energy passages transform into moments of calm and restraint.

It is unusual for Higdon to present a large portion of text in a relatively small section of music, yet here she chooses to do so. Over measures 104–119, the text is

And into that gate they shall enter, And in that house they shall dwell, Where there shall be no cloud nor sun, no darkness nor dazzling, but one equal light, No noise nor silence, But one equal music.

The choir, again nearly a cappella, returns to the work's opening chant-like motives moving in parallel and stepwise motion. This texture is coupled with alternating major and minor modes: E minor–E major–E minor–F♯ minor–G major–F♯ minor–E major, as shown in Figure 3-10. The result recalls medieval music, which is an evident source of influence.

While the musical phrases and subphrases thus far have been brief, containing succinct, rhythmic melodies and sometimes melodic fragments, in measures 103–119 the lines and rhythms elongate. The choir sings sustained melodies that paint the text through a gradual stepwise arch. The contour rises on the word "enter," rises again for "in that house" (a metaphor for heaven), and descends on the last words in the phrase, "they shall dwell."

Higdon cadences on E♭ major only two times in this work—once in measure 119 on the word "music" (Donne's metaphor for God's presence in heaven) and later in measure 215 on "the house of God." An E♭ major cadence is thus associated with paradise.

Figure 3-10. Jennifer Higdon, *On the Death of the Righteous*, mm. 104–119
Music Copyright © 2008 by Jennifer Higdon [ASCAP].
Text by John Donne.

Development Section

Measures 128–178 become, for their length, developmental procedures, and musical complexities, the centerpiece of the composition. This development accounts for approximately 16 percent of the piece. It is crafted in five sections connected by motivic unity and a repetition of text originally found in measures 48–79, threaded with brief connecting orchestral interludes. There are a number of tonal center allusions, and the harmonic rhythm is rapid. The shifting tonal centers at times offer calm and repose, at other times surprise, and at still other times assurance and triumph. The shifts force the listener's ear to adjust moment by moment in intricate consort with the words.

While the harmonies shift frequently even within measures, the centering tonalities in the five sections contained within this developmental portion are as follows:

Section 1, mm. 128–133: starts on E♭ major (m. 128, beat 4) and migrates to F major

Section 2, mm. 134–137: choir joins on B♭ (m. 136) and moves to C major (m. 137)

Section 3, mm. 137–155: C major (mm. 137–145), D major spelled enharmonically with G♭ in place of F♯ (m. 148 beat 3), D♭ major (m. 149 beat 3 to m. 150), B♭ major (m. 151 beat 3), return to C major (mm. 155+)

Section 4, mm. 157–164: C minor (m. 157 beat 4) to A minor (m. 158), alternating A minor and A major (mm. 158–161), migrating through triads of A♭, C, F, and G (m. 162–163), and culminating in a framing tonality of A major (m. 164)

Section 5, mm. 166–178: G major, planing through triads and returning to A major (m. 178)

The harmonic volatility is readily apparent. Over the entire development, the tonality progresses a tritone in key relationships; E♭ major and A major become the framing tonal centers, even though these tonalities do not share pitches in the overtone series. Figure 3-11 shows these framing tonal centers.

Figure 3-11. Jennifer Higdon, *On the Death of the Righteous*,
mm. 128–129 and 178
Music Copyright © 2008 by Jennifer Higdon [ASCAP].
Text by John Donne.

Higdon repeats in measures 166–178 (Figure 3-12) text that was initially found in measures 64–70. The choir's pitches and the parallel triads are repeated exactly from their first appearance, but the rhythm is twice as long, creating gravity through elongation. The text painting is also identical to the setting in measures 64–70, with the one exception already discussed. In measure 69, Higdon moved from A major into A minor on the word "Glory"; now in measure 178 she gives assurance to the word by remaining in A major. The conclusion of this section is, musically and poetically, a glorious high point of the work; it creates an overwhelming sense of uplift and arrival.

Figure 3-12. Jennifer Higdon, *On the Death of the Righteous*, mm. 172–178
Music Copyright © 2008 by Jennifer Higdon [ASCAP].
Text by John Donne.

Final Instrumental Interlude

Higdon typically follows a climax with an immediate segue to the ending, but in *On the Death of the Righteous*, she follows the climax with the longest, most developed section of orchestral writing in the entire work. This interlude spans measures 179–199 and is truly an orchestral statement in which Higdon uses her skills as an orchestral composer to bring intensity to the poetic drama. The texture is rhythmically dense, homorhythmic at times and contrapuntal at others. This interlude is transitional and harmonically vague; polytonal allusions appear in the orchestra during measures 186–188 and measures 195–197, for example.

Why write the longest, most highly developed orchestral section immediately following the work's choral and poetic climax? And what, if anything, does this have to do with the music–text relationship?

The choir has just sung of an ultimate spiritual victory of awaking in God's glory. The orchestra extends the climatic power of this image. It continues to elaborate and intensify Donne's sermon, much like an organ interlude that follows the sermon in a worship service. This moment provides a period of reflection before the conclusion of the ceremony or, in this case, the work.

This particular interlude also unifies the piece by incorporating musical devices from throughout the work. These devices include harmonic parallelism, root movements by half steps, a series of exposed tritones— articulated in accented trills occurring at cadence points—and scalar passages.

Figure 3-13, taken from the reduction in the choral score, highlights a slice of this interlude. The lower voices feature broken counterpoint with abrupt shifts between major and minor modes, which hint at B major or Mixolydian. The upper voices often employ parallel chordal structures, using smaller rhythmic values. While Higdon rarely uses a strict, octatonic passage, one occurs in measure 183. Rapidly ascending instrumental flourishes continue to build this section, as in measure 183 voiced in the trumpets and violas, and in measure 184 set in the violins and woodwinds.

Figure 3-13. Jennifer Higdon, *On the Death of the Righteous*, mm. 182–187
Music Copyright © 2008 by Jennifer Higdon [ASCAP].

These devices convey anything but peaceful resolve, conclusion, or triumphant victory. They bring angst, instability, and restlessness. The orchestration creates a strong expectation that another climax can be anticipated when the choir reenters; however, no such climax will come. Higdon seems to use the angst as a musical metaphor for a theme that Donne refers to often in his writings: the struggles of human life and the need for spiritual relief from them.

The interlude concludes in measures 198–199 (Figure 3-14). Simultaneous tonal centers on E major and G major abruptly shift to parallel G major and A major triads without a conclusive cadence.

Figure 3-14. Jennifer Higdon, *On the Death of the Righteous*, mm. 198–200
Music Copyright © 2008 by Jennifer Higdon [ASCAP].
Text by John Donne.

Closing Section

As the orchestral flurry releases, the sopranos emerge from the background as if from another world (Figure 3-15). Their entrance is almost imperceptibly threaded through the dense, nervous orchestral fabric, and provides absolute serenity as the orchestra drops out.

Other voices join in descending stacked secundal lines, weaving downward from the suspended soprano tone. The allusion to D Dorian creates a mystical context for the final statement of the text "They shall awake, and they shall say, Surely the Lord is in this place." This treatment is starkly different from the text's first treatment in measures 14–21, in which it was built up through ascending lines with added seconds climbing to a discordant cadence.

In measures 208–211, the text setting of "Surely the Lord is in this place" is now calming and assuring, by virtue of its gentle downward motion, consonant triadic harmony, and relative absence of coloring extensions and seconds. With the orchestra still silent, the texture is lean, transparent, even angelic. Higdon creates a sense of calm through progressively augmenting note values from sixteenth notes to eighth notes to quarter notes and finally to half notes and a cadence that lasts for five beats on the word "place."

Figure 3-15. Jennifer Higdon, *On the Death of the Righteous*, mm. 199–211
Music Copyright © 2008 by Jennifer Higdon [ASCAP].
Text by John Donne.

The chimes enter in measure 211, overlapping the choir with a simple, descending motive in B♭ Lydian. The instrument's religious association and the descent of its melody facilitate a sense of sacred repose. Over measures 211–215 (Figure 3-16), Higdon employs counterpoint on the text "and this no other but the house of God." The defining E♮s of B♭ Lydian mode create associations of brightness, reflecting the joy in the text. This imitative section cadences on an E♭ major triad in measure 215, the lines relaxing downward to a quiet cadence on the phrase "the house of God." This is the piece's second cadence on E♭ major, after the cadence in measure 119 which arrived on the ascending climactic point on the word "music," used by Donne as a metaphor for God's presence in heaven.

Figure 3-16. Jennifer Higdon, *On the Death of the Righteous*, mm. 211–215
Music Copyright © 2008 by Jennifer Higdon [ASCAP].
Text by John Donne.

Over measures 215–217 (Figure 3-17) on the text "and the gate of heaven," the musical effect is startling, soulful, and expressive, made possible by root movement as the basses rise gently from E♭ major to a tritone away on A major. Similar tritone harmonic root movement occurred over measures 199–210, in that instance going from E major to B♭ major, another tritone.

Figure 3-17. Jennifer Higdon, *On the Death of the Righteous*, mm. 215–217
Music Copyright © 2008 by Jennifer Higdon [ASCAP].
Text by John Donne.

In measures 218–222 (Figure 3-18), the sopranos, altos, and tenors return to the earlier text, "Keep us Lord so awake in the duties of our callings." In measures 166–178, this text was sung in rhythmic augmentation as compared with its first appearance in measures 64–79. Now the rhythm is varied and further augmented, and the three voices sing in parallel motion. It is clear that through this rhythmic variance, the music is winding down to the end; with this descent and rhythmic augmentation, the righteous represented in Donne's text are reaching a point of accepting, and easing into, their callings.

Figure 3-18. Jennifer Higdon, *On the Death of the Righteous*, mm. 218–222
Music Copyright © 2008 by Jennifer Higdon [ASCAP].
Text by John Donne.

As the three upper voices intone "that we may thus sleep in Thy peace, and wake in Thy Glory" (Figure 3-19), they move in mostly parallel motion in a series of half and whole steps. The harmony alternates major and minor triads. The contour paints the same motion as the text, descending and then rising again. Beginning in measure 218 (see Figure 3-18 above) until the final cadence, the basses chant on a unison C pedal tone the title of the poem, "On the Death of the Righteous." They undergird the foundational thought for the entire composition. The chanting becomes so compelling that the other voices ultimately succumb and join the C major chord. On the penultimate word of the work, "Glory," the harmony arrives on the pure tonality of C major, which has earlier been associated with the idea of communion; see, for example, measure 142. The use of C major here implies the idea that the saints will experience community when arriving in God's glory.

Figure 3-19. Jennifer Higdon, *On the Death of the Righteous*, mm. 223–300
Music Copyright © 2008 by Jennifer Higdon [ASCAP].
Text by John Donne.

This closing is marked again with the chimes. Adding to the religious references, the final "Amen" occurs on a plagal cadence, a closing formula so common in traditional church music that it is known as the "amen cadence." Higdon does not use such a cadence in any of her other choral works. What then inspired her to use one here? Donne's original text does not include an "Amen"; Higdon chose to add it. When asked why she closed the work in such a traditional fashion, she responded, "I am not sure why I chose that kind of cadence there; I was not aware I had done that." It is clear that Higdon does much of her work instinctively, instead of intentionally selecting musical devices to set text. This is, perhaps, a mark of her genius.

Concluding Remarks

Scored to accompany Verdi's *Requiem*, *On the Death of the Righteous* is, in some ways, on a parallel plane with the iconic nineteenth-century Italian masterpiece. Though lasting a modest twelve minutes, the piece displays a variety of musical contrasts comparable to those found in the ninety-minute *Requiem*. It is both grandiose and intimate, spanning an enormous range of musical, poetic, and spiritual expression. The quiet intimacy in this score draws the audience in; contrasting dense and powerful sections overwhelm them. *On the Death of the Righteous* is a serious and refined choral-orchestral work, demanding moments of introspection and mystical reflection.

Higdon honors Donne's text with a fresh artistic voice. Her setting reveals the text's spiritual leanings in a manner that speaks to modern-day performers and audiences. She gives Donne's words intelligent support in the instrumentation. In almost every moment, the musical devices are implicitly connected to the text. It is rare to find sections that are purely music for music's sake, that is, having no symbolic relevance to the words. Repeated text is often given contrasting musical treatment, and the same text achieves different meanings through different musical settings. Particular chords are used as quasi-leitmotivic harmonies for particular text concepts; these aurally identify key words, phrases, and ideas through consistent harmonies. For example, Eb major appears on references to the presence of God in measures 119 and 215. C major appears on the word "music" in measure 48, on a resolute cadence on the word "communion" in measure 142, and then under the text "no foes nor friends" in measures 144–146. Each of these passages emphasizes egalitarianism, unity, and living in community.

To express the traditional, religious nature of Donne's text, Higdon incorporates medieval or Renaissance musical references through modal writing, stepwise parallel homophony, austere chant-like motives, and sparce orchestration. The sections using these techniques return intermittently to unify the work and ground the listener.

Donne's text describes a life that is filled with troubles, trials, and difficulties until one awakes, hears, and answers God's call. Throughout *On the Death of the Righteous*, Higdon's music represents the challenging and mysterious struggles that arise in the course of life. It is a meaningful artistic offering for a twenty-first-century audience.

The piece is challenging to perform since it requires enormous performance forces in one moment and chamber music voices in the next. But the challenge is worth accepting, and the result is well worth the effort.

CHAPTER FOUR

RUMINATIONS

Ruminations
(2016) 17 minutes
Chamber ensemble (total of 12 players), SATB chorus
1,1 (doubling bass clarinet),1,1,1, hp.,
1 perc, 2 violins, 1 viola, 1 cello, 1 contrabass
Text by Rumi, translation by Coleman Barks, spiritual

Commissioned by the Washington Master Chorale
(made possible by a grant from the National Endowment for the Arts and a
private gift in memory of Denny Clark)
and the Rhodes College Endowment
(made possible by a bequest from John Murray Springfield '51)

Ruminations, whose creative title was chosen by Higdon, has seven movements using six poems and a quotation attributed to Rumi, the thirteenth-century Persian poet, expert in Islamic law, theologian, and Sufi mystic. The work is meant to be performed in its entirety. From a musical standpoint, it is possible to perform movements individually, but doing so will interrupt the overarching effects of the poetry. It is ultimately an artistic decision for the conductor.

Choral and solo movements alternate in this work: movements one, three, five, and seven are choruses, while two, four, and six feature solo singers. The number of soloists increases for each successive movement: movement two is a duet, movement four a trio, and movement six a quartet.

Higdon composed *Ruminations* in 2016 on a dual commission from the Washington Master Chorale and the Rhodes College Endowment. According to its publisher Lawdon Press, one of the commissioning bodies desired a text that was nonreligious, while the other preferred a spiritual but not necessarily religious text. As the text would inspire Higdon's musical setting, its selection was paramount. In the end, all parties agreed on selected writings of Rumi. The poems are reproduced in this book with the kind permission of Coleman Barks, translator of *The Essential Rumi*.[1]

Given the personal and meditative quality of Rumi's writings, the aesthetic desires of the commissioning groups, and performance resources, Higdon wrote for chamber orchestra rather than full orchestra. The size of the chorus can be modest or large, as long as the singers can meet the work's high technical demands.

I. Water from Your Spring (c. 3′10″)

What was in that candle's light
that opened up and consumed me so quickly?

Come back, my friend! The form of our love
is not a created form.

Nothing can help me but that beauty.
There was a dawn I remember

when my soul heard something
from your soul. I drank water

from your spring and felt
the current take me.

Rumi, in translation by Coleman Barks

[reproduced with permission]

With a four-measure orchestral introduction, Higdon creates an ethereal atmosphere that animates Rumi's words before they occur. The strings enter in stacked seconds marked *fp* and sustained. The woodwinds play overlaying hairpin effects (crescendos and decrescendos) also voiced in seconds. Ambient percussion affects are achieved through offbeat entrances and unpredictable rhythms played by the glockenspiel, crotales struck with knitting needles, and the harp in harmonics. Figure 4-1a illustrates the attention that Higdon has given to create such a moment.

---

[1]   *The Essential Rumi*, ed. and trans. Coleman Barks (San Francisco: HarperCollins, 2004).

Figure 4-1a. Jennifer Higdon, *Ruminations*: "Water from Your Spring," mm. 1–4
Music Copyright © 2016 by Jennifer Higdon [ASCAP].

The work is unified by motives that appear in both the orchestra and chorus. The first of these is a syncopated, whole-tone ascent in the trumpet's opening statement in measures 2–4. This line is then alluded to by the chorus in its first statement. The motive will be vividly recalled again by the trumpet in the measure immediately preceding the final movement. Other recurring motives are the descending line in measures 4–5, scored here in harp and double bass, and the sixteenth- and eighth-note rhythm in the trumpet and upper strings in measure 5 (Figure 4-1b). Throughout the movement, the latter motive represents the animated flicker of a candle's light. For example, in measures 5 and 9, it surrounds the text mentioning light in measure 7. In both occurrences, the motive is set in the strings playing stacked seconds in high harmonics.

The choir begins in a quasi C Lydian mode for the text "What was in that candle's light that opened and consumed me so quickly?" Their line oscillates briefly around F♯ and then rises to an E by measure 9. The rhythms underscore the text with a sense of urgency: on the first syllable of "consumed" and on the word "quickly," the choir uses a dotted rhythm borrowed from the orchestra.

Figure 4-1b. Jennifer Higdon, *Ruminations*: "Water from Your Spring," mm. 1–10
Music Copyright © 2016 by Jennifer Higdon [ASCAP].
Rumi texts translated by Coleman Barks and used with permission.

    After a two-measure bridge in the vibraphone, a semi-syncopated
sixteenth- and eighth-note ostinato appears in the instrumentation in
measure 15 (Figure 4-2). The choir returns in measure 16 with the text
"Come back, my friend," which is set in the upper three voices on a B
major triad, continuing the semi-syncopated motive. The basses quickly
echo the plea on insistent eighth notes.

Figure 4-2. Jennifer Higdon, *Ruminations*: "Water from Your Spring," mm. 15–17
Music Copyright © 2016 by Jennifer Higdon [ASCAP].
Rumi texts translated by Coleman Barks and used with permission.

The passage in measures 18–22 (Figure 4-3), "The form of our love is not a created form," is stepwise, with the exception of a leap on the word "created," accentuating the importance of a created form. The male voices take up the text "Nothing can help me but that beauty," and incorporate the ostinato from the orchestra. On the word "beauty," the female voices join the resolution on a B major triad. This resolution emphasizes the warm, soothing beauty of the lover's form.

Figure 4-3. Jennifer Higdon, *Ruminations*: "Water from Your Spring," mm. 18–22
Music Copyright © 2016 by Jennifer Higdon [ASCAP].
Rumi texts translated by Coleman Barks and used with permission.

In measures 25–26 (Figure 4-4), as the singers recall an earlier time with the text "There was a dawn, I remember," the opening vocal motive returns. The line continues "when my soul heard something from your soul." This soul-to-soul connection is depicted through a rising movement conveying a sense of euphoria. The orchestra continues to deliver the semi-syncopated rhythm that unifies the work; the light motive is also heard when remembering the light of dawn. The chorus resolves on the word "soul" and establishes the frequent use of B major as a home tone.

Bridging to the next section, the strings again play the light motive. A brief, ascending sixteenth-note passage, seen in Figure 4-4 mm. 27–28, recalls the opening trumpet line, repeated here in rhythmic diminution, again played by the trumpet. In measure 29, the light motive is seen once again.

Figure 4-4. Jennifer Higdon, *Ruminations*: "Water from Your Spring," mm. 25–29
Music Copyright © 2016 by Jennifer Higdon [ASCAP].
Rumi texts translated by Coleman Barks and used with permission.

Higdon sets the concluding text, "I drank water from your spring and felt the current take me," on an arched contour (Figure 4-5); the line descends on the text "drank water from the spring," and ascends on "and felt the current take me." This melodic shape, along with sixteenth and dotted-eighth rhythms, conveys a sense of the current's motion.

The male voices repeat a fragment of the phrase, "I drank water from your spring," to a marvelous, soul-calming effect. The basses represent the spring's depth, while the tenors depict its movement through subtly rising and returning to the definitive F♯ of C Lydian that opened the work. The tenor and bass slow into longer rhythms, and rests interrupt and delay the text. A sense of hesitation and suspense leaves the audience questioning: what is going to happen next? Thin, secundal writing in the lower strings couches the male voices. Through a descending line and tumbling rhythmic motive, the orchestra paints the image of running water from a spring.

The poetry in this movement expresses the intense intimacy experienced in deep human-to-human, soul-to-soul connection, as well as in an individual's connection to the spiritual aspects of life.

Figure 4-5. Jennifer Higdon, *Ruminations*: "Water from Your Spring," mm. 33–40
Music Copyright © 2016 by Jennifer Higdon [ASCAP].
Rumi texts translated by Coleman Barks and used with permission.

II. Today, Like Every Other Day (c. 2′)

Today, like every other day, we wake up empty
and frightened. Don't open the door to the study
and begin reading. Take down a musical instrument.

Let the beauty we love be what we do.
There are hundreds of ways to kneel and kiss the ground.

Rumi, in translation by Coleman Barks

[reproduced with permission]

In this lyrical duet, Rumi's writing is delicately set in two solo female voices with chamber instruments. The seven-measure opening incorporates the offbeat rhythm of the first movement's opening trumpet motive, now set in the flute and violas (Figure 4-6). The solo second violin joins in a rocking motion, while the first violin plays open fifths. The violins collectively outline the C Lydian mode that opened the work and connects this movement to the first. The rocking motion is an aural representation of an ordinary, somewhat humdrum day, with the constant ticking of a clock and the slow passing of time.

Figure 4-6. Jennifer Higdon, *Ruminations*:
"Today, Like Every Other Day," mm. 41–46
Music Copyright © 2016 by Jennifer Higdon [ASCAP].
Rumi texts translated by Coleman Barks and used with permission.

Higdon sets the soprano and alto lines in conversation, the alto beginning in the sixteenth and dotted-eighth rhythm seen in the first movement (Figure 4-7). The soprano follows in counterpoint, repeating the same rhythmic motive on the word "other." The voices continue in C Lydian, now with a raised fifth scale degree, G♯. The alto then speeds up into sixteenth notes on the text "every other day." Though the day is described as routine and ordinary, the unusual modal writing, the quick–slow rhythm, and the counterpoint generate uncertainty. The text continues, "we wake up empty and frightened." The quick–slow rhythm appears again on the words "wake up," suggesting a sudden and anxious waking. The voices merge then separate in contrary motion, landing on an interval of a minor seventh on "frightened." Coloring the unsettled, troubled progression of this movement are minor sevenths, seconds, and tritones set against more reassuring perfect fifths.

Figure 4-7. Jennifer Higdon, *Ruminations*:
"Today, Like Every Other Day," mm. 47–51
Music Copyright © 2016 by Jennifer Higdon [ASCAP].
Rumi texts translated by Coleman Barks and used with permission.

The text beginning in measure 54 (Figure 4-8) is "Don't open the door to the study and begin reading … Take down a musical instrument." It seems to be a warning not to take time for granted, but instead to relish every moment as an opportunity to find beauty through music. The voices move lyrically but in subtly disjunct counterpoint, as on the words "the study" in measure 55 and "reading" in measure 58. Unmatching rhythms lend momentary instability, especially as the lines often move in contrary rather than parallel motion.

Figure 4-8. Jennifer Higdon, *Ruminations*: "Today, Like Every Other Day," mm. 54–62
Music Copyright © 2016 by Jennifer Higdon [ASCAP].
Rumi texts translated by Coleman Barks and used with permission.

Rumi's words become more uplifting on the text "Let the beauty we love be what we do" (Figure 4-9). The voices rise and crescendo, generating an impression of souls rising together and finding bliss in this otherwise troubled day.

Figure 4-9. Jennifer Higdon, *Ruminations*: "Today, Like Every Other Day," mm. 64–66
Music Copyright © 2016 by Jennifer Higdon [ASCAP].
Rumi texts translated by Coleman Barks and used with permission.

The conversation between alto and soprano finishes with the line "There are hundreds of ways to kneel and kiss the ground." The soprano responds to the alto in descending motives on "kneel and kiss the ground." In measure 72, the flute anticipates the descending motive before the text is sung for the last time. The orchestra briefly returns to the gliding, rocking motion that opened this section before also playing a descending line to end the movement (Figure 4-10).

Figure 4-10. Jennifer Higdon, *Ruminations*:
"Today, Like Every Other Day," mm. 73–78
Music Copyright © 2016 by Jennifer Higdon [ASCAP].
Rumi texts translated by Coleman Barks and used with permission.

The harmony in measure 76 cadences on a B^9 chord, a reference to B Lydian. Over the entire movement, the harmony moves downward by a simple half step, beginning in C Lydian and ending in B Lydian. This could very well be another reference to kneeling to the ground, or simply a symbol of the small progression of the day. This second musical vignette has asked listeners to pause and savor the moment.

III. Drum (c. 3′30″)

In this drumbeat moment of red flowers opening
and grapes being crushed,
the soul and luminous clarity sit together.

All desire wants is a taste of you,
two small villages in a mountain valley
where everyone longs for presence.

We start to step up.
A step appears.

You say, I am more compassionate
than your mother and father.

I made medicine out of your pain.
From your chimney smoke I shape new constellations.

I tell everything, but I do not say it,
because my friend, it is better
your secret be spoken by you.

Rumi, in translation by Coleman Barks

[reproduced with permission]

    The darker and more aggressive third movement is a stark contrast to the preceding movement. The six-measure orchestral introduction is scored for the low strings, bass clarinet, the lower tessitura of the harp and horn, and a hand-beaten bass drum that provides a driving tribal character throughout the movement. In the fourth measure, the drum introduces an ostinato consisting of an alternation of one eighth and two sixteenth notes over the 12/8 meter (see Figure 4-11). This rhythm, excited though it may be, is related to the soft, cerebral trumpet solo that opened the work, with ties and offbeats riding over the top. Additional instruments enter in broken and hocket-like rhythms. Polyrhythms, particularly three against two, create a sense of instability and threat. Harmonic cross-relations of B versus B♭ amplify this intensity, leading to the entrance for male voices.

Figure 4-11. Jennifer Higdon, *Ruminations*: "Drum," mm. 79–82
Music Copyright © 2016 by Jennifer Higdon [ASCAP].

The voices enter with the text "In this drumbeat, moments of red flowers opening and grapes being crushed." They move against the triple meter with a duple rhythm on the word "drumbeat" to accentuate the word's meaning (Figure 4-12). The two lines begin in unison and separate in oblique motion, as if painting the opening of the flowers. B♮s in the orchestra clash with the established G minor harmony on the word "crushed."

The text changes to elevated subject matter as "the soul and luminous clarity sit together." Here the melody rises as the altos and sopranos join in measures 89 and 90, respectively. Momentary ease is created by a consonant G major triad under the word "clarity."

Figure 4-12. Jennifer Higdon, *Ruminations*: "Drum," mm. 85–91
Music Copyright © 2016 by Jennifer Higdon [ASCAP].
Rumi texts translated by Coleman Barks and used with permission.

On the text "All desire wants is a taste of you, two small villages in a mountain valley where everyone longs for presence," the male voices again begin in unison, but they move in escalating seconds to the word "desire." Higdon inserts a slight pause before repeating "all desire," now with the female voices intensifying the sense of longing. The voices surge to a peak on "is a taste of you" and convey a hunger to connect, to taste another soul or a greater being. The two small villages serve as a metaphor for two souls. Higdon stretches the choir's rhythm on these words, and on the word "presence" in measure 100, using a duple set against triplets as in the choir's first phrase (Figure 4-13a). This rhythmic elongation in homophonic dotted-quarter notes emphasizes the longing for such presence. The word "presence" arrives on a climactic F major triad in a high vocal tessitura, and the listener is swept into a musically overcoming *ff* cadence. This high point arrives without warning, rendering any defenses useless. The desire for presence is all consuming.

Figure 4-13a. Jennifer Higdon, *Ruminations*: "Drum," mm. 96–100
Music Copyright © 2016 by Jennifer Higdon [ASCAP].
Rumi texts translated by Coleman Barks and used with permission.

A dynamic six-measure orchestral bridge extends the experience of this searching, longing euphoria before the next section of poetry. The bridge begins on the pedal tone F, with F major in the upper orchestra and choral resolution, and ends in B, a tritone away (Figure 4-13b). At this moment, the poetry moves from a longing for presence to the next line, "We start to step up," which points to an approach toward that presence. On the text "We start to step up. A step appears," the step occurs musically as the voices move stepwise upward.

Figure 4-13b. Jennifer Higdon, *Ruminations*: "Drum," mm. 100–108
Music Copyright © 2016 by Jennifer Higdon [ASCAP].
Rumi texts translated by Coleman Barks and used with permission.

   The choir incorporates duple figures on the words (italicized here) "*I
am* more compassionate than your *mother* and *father*" (Figure 4-13c).
These duple rhythms add gravitas to these words against the otherwise
constant triplets. Now in open fifths, the choir sings "I make medicine out
of your pain," though a minor triad colors the word "pain." According to
Rumi's texts, pain must be the key to conversion and soulful connection
with the other. The instrumentation is minimal in this moment, but on the
text "From your chimney smoke I shape new constellations," the full
orchestra enters for profound impact, a metaphor for creation. A five-
measure bridge ensues, continuing the forward momentum.

Figure 4-13c. Jennifer Higdon, *Ruminations*: "Drum," mm. 109–115
Music Copyright © 2016 by Jennifer Higdon [ASCAP].
Rumi texts translated by Coleman Barks and used with permission.

In longer, sustained tones, rather than the small note values that began other sections, the female voices sing, "I tell everything, but I do not say it." The men echo the women in imitative counterpoint, which is used, along with intermittent rests, to create anticipation and suspense. As the movement comes to an end with the words "because my friend, it is better your secret be spoken by you," the rhythms are broken, delayed, and elongated (Figure 4-14); there is hesitation in the music. Long note values, increased use of duplets against triplets, and rests between segments of poetry stretch out time and convey a thoughtfulness about the way the text is expressed.

The ostinato in the orchestra also stretches in rhythm, relaxes, and finally settles with the choir's cadence. The drums are now silent. Only the strings surround the choir in accepting resolve as a descending lyric melody transitions to the next movement.

Figure 4-14. Jennifer Higdon, *Ruminations*: "Drum," mm. 128–135
Music Copyright © 2016 by Jennifer Higdon [ASCAP].
Rumi texts translated by Coleman Barks and used with permission.

IV. All Day and Night (c. 2′)

All day and night, music,
a quiet, bright
reedsong. If it
fades, we fade.

Rumi, in translation by Coleman Barks

[reproduced with permission]

"All Day and Night" features alto, tenor, and bass soloists, but also incorporates the chorus in a role that blends into the orchestration. Connecting this movement to the preceding movement, the chorus continues to phonate the vowel "ooo" from the previous movement's last word, "you." They hold the home tonality of E♭, regardless of the surrounding tonalities. The movement opens with unpredictable and quasi-pointillistic orchestration, as separately articulated pitches in the woodwinds and brass intersect and join (Figure 4-15a). This texture repeats in variation throughout the movement. Punctuations come from a lightly brushed mark tree in the percussion.

Figure 4-15a. Jennifer Higdon, *Ruminations*: "All Day and Night," mm. 134–138
Music Copyright © 2016 by Jennifer Higdon [ASCAP].

Spaciousness and a suspension in time are created through exposed, naked, interwoven instrumental lines. This impressionistic movement is similar to the second movement in textures and transparency. The second began with a soloistic, contrapuntal rocking, gliding motion in the strings; here a string trio collaborates with the soloists, establishing intimacy and delicacy in a balladic conversation. Also like the second movement, "Today, Like Every Other Day," the text of "All Day and Night, Music" shares the theme of a single day.

The soloists have staggered entrances, each slightly altered rhythmically in exposed counterpoint (Figure 4-15b). They end on quintal chords that couch the text "All day and night, music, A quiet bright reedsong."

Figure 4-15b. Jennifer Higdon, *Ruminations*: "All Day and Night," mm. 143–147
Music Copyright © 2016 by Jennifer Higdon [ASCAP].
Rumi texts translated by Coleman Barks and used with permission.

Measures 149–157 are decidedly impressionistic. Harmonies move slowly, colored by quartal, quintal, and secundal chords (Figure 4-16). The effect is austere serenity.

Figure 4-16. Jennifer Higdon, *Ruminations*: "All Day and Night," mm. 147–157
Music Copyright © 2016 by Jennifer Higdon [ASCAP].
Rumi texts translated by Coleman Barks and used with permission.

After a five-measure orchestral bridge, the bass, tenor, and alto reenter in turn (Figure 4-17). These rising vocal timbres raise the possibility that "If it [the music] fades, we fade." The orchestra drops out, and the ending of the movement, measures 168–171, is a cappella. The soloists repeat the phrase of text with subtle rhythmic variances that suggest apprehension and uncertainty. Higdon continues the descending line that opened the movement, altered through slight rhythmic metamorphosis. The soloists fade out one by one; disconcertingly, the bass voice finishes alone on E, a tritone from the tenor's last note, Bb.

If the music fades, we fade—is Rumi hinting that music is a spiritual life force?

Figure 4-17. Jennifer Higdon, *Ruminations*: "All Day and Night," mm. 165–171
Music Copyright © 2016 by Jennifer Higdon [ASCAP].
Rumi texts translated by Coleman Barks and used with permission.

V. Where Everything Is Music (c. 3′30″)

Don't worry about saving these songs!
And if one of our instruments breaks,
it doesn't matter.

We have fallen into the place
where everything is music.

The strumming and the flute notes
rise into the atmosphere,
and even if the whole world's harp
should burn up, there will still be
hidden instruments playing.

So the candle flickers and goes out.
We have a piece of flint, and a spark.

This singing art is sea foam.
The graceful movements come from a pearl
somewhere on the ocean floor.

Poems reach up like spindrift and the edge
of driftwood along the beach, wanting!

They derive
from a slow and powerful root
that we can't see.

Stop the words now.
Open the window in the center of your chest,
and let the spirits fly in and out.

Rumi, in translation by Coleman Barks

[reproduced with permission]

Higdon has reserved the fifth poem, "Where Everything Is Music," for the golden moment of the composition. The poem emphasizes a connection between art, music, spirituality, and life. Music is a theme in all of the Rumi poems Higdon selected, as it is in Jeanne Minahan's poetry for *The Singing Rooms* and John Donne's sermon for *The Death of the Righteous*.

The movement begins with a new sixteenth- and eighth-note rhythmic pattern in the lower woodwinds and weaving sixteenth notes in the harp; these rhythms represent the worry or underlying anxieties in daily life. Their patterns at first outline D minor (Figure 4-18), but F♯s appear in cross-related secundal utterances and soon bring the tonality into D major. The vibraphone strikes quintal chords over measures 173–174. The strings play a portamento crescendo, sliding from one secundal chord in measure 174 to another, *ff,* in measure 175, creating a gleefully eerie effect. Portamentos in the strings become a defining feature of this movement. All of the instrumentation serves to contradict the idea of fading from the previous movement.

Where Everything Is Music

Figure 4-18. Jennifer Higdon, *Ruminations*:
"Where Everything Is Music," mm. 172–175
Music Copyright © 2016 by Jennifer Higdon [ASCAP].

The opening line is "Don't worry about saving these songs, And if one of our instruments breaks, it doesn't matter." Rumi counsels listeners not to be anxious, even though the music itself indicates some level of anxiety. Rumi insists that even if an instrument breaks, the music—a metaphor for life—will continue. On "our instruments break," B♮ breaks the key of what would otherwise be D minor and brings the harmony of D Dorian. In measure 189, the strings' portamentos (see Figure 4-19a) anticipate the perception of falling in the text "we have fallen into that place where everything is music." After several measures of D Dorian, the word "music" cadences triumphantly with a D major triad on the downbeat of measure 192 (Figure 4-19b).

Figure 4-19a. Jennifer Higdon, *Ruminations*:
"Where Everything Is Music," m. 189
Music Copyright © 2016 by Jennifer Higdon [ASCAP].

Figure 4-19b. Jennifer Higdon, *Ruminations*:
"Where Everything Is Music," mm. 190–193
Music Copyright © 2016 by Jennifer Higdon [ASCAP].
Rumi texts translated by Coleman Barks and used with permission.

In the next fragment, "The strumming and the flute notes rise into the atmosphere," strumming is anticipated in strumming chords from the harp and violin; "the flute notes" are followed by florid passages in the flute in measures 198–199 (Figure 4-20). The male voices sing the first phrase and are joined by the female voices as the dynamic builds to a *mf* in a burst of sound on "rise into the atmosphere." The flute descends in another florid passage in measure 201.

Figure 4-20. Jennifer Higdon, *Ruminations*:
"Where Everything Is Music," mm. 197–201
Music Copyright © 2016 by Jennifer Higdon [ASCAP].
Rumi texts translated by Coleman Barks and used with permission.

Higdon incorporates numerous stacked seconds in the text "and even if the whole world's harp should burn up, there will be hidden instruments playing" (Figure 4-21). She brilliantly delays the cadence with melodic descent, elongated rhythmic values, thinning voices, and rests. The voices pause for a quarter rest before arriving on the word "playing." The instruments are now in eighth notes rather than sixteenth notes.

Figure 4-21. Jennifer Higdon, *Ruminations*:
"Where Everything Is Music," pickup to mm. 202–206
Music Copyright © 2016 by Jennifer Higdon [ASCAP].
Rumi texts translated by Coleman Barks and used with permission.

The female voices reenter on "So, a candle that flickers and goes out." This flickering is depicted musically as the rhythm indeed flickers on an offbeat. "We have a piece of flint, and a spark" is marked with a sudden crescendo before a decrescendo begins onomatopoeically on the word "spark" in measure 211 (Figure 4-22). A clashing C♯ minor/B polychord is struck at the same moment. After the choir sings "This singing art is sea foam," the orchestra bridges with descending lines in measure 212, and the string portamentos return in measure 214, in imitation of the motion and cohesion of sea foam.

Figure 4-22. Jennifer Higdon, *Ruminations*: "Where Everything Is Music," mm. 209–214
Music Copyright © 2016 by Jennifer Higdon [ASCAP].
Rumi texts translated by Coleman Barks and used with permission.

A two-measure instrumental break leads into the movement's peak. The voices enter in eight-part divisi and parallel motion (Figure 4-23). Graceful eighth notes are predominant on the text "The graceful movements come from a pearl somewhere on the ocean floor." The word "movements" is painted by a whole-step rise from Eb Mixolydian to an F minor seventh chord. The pearl found on the ocean floor settles on a Bb major triad.

Figure 4-23. Jennifer Higdon, *Ruminations*:
"Where Everything Is Music," mm. 214–216
Music Copyright © 2016 by Jennifer Higdon [ASCAP].
Rumi texts translated by Coleman Barks and used with permission.

In the next phrase, "Poems reach up like spindrift and the edge of driftwood along a beach, wanting!" the sense of deep want is described by the rising vocal melody and elongated note values (Figure 4-24). Ascending through Bb Mixolydian, the music partially cadences on an Eb triad in measures 220–221 yet surges to an Ab^9 chord in measure 222 for a true cadence and peak. The orchestra's rhythmic motion becomes vertical, as every beat takes on the insistence of a downbeat, replacing the more complex rhythms that have characterized the orchestration to this point. This emphasizes the text "They derived from a slow and powerful root that we can't see." Through insistence on each beat, the orchestra drives home the image of a "powerful root." In the choir, the word "root" is grounded with a half note and rest. They also sing half notes rising in parallel motion to "can't see." As the following instrumental bridge sounds festive and celebratory, the music seems to offer hope that the "powerful root that we can't see" might eventually be seen musically and that wanting might be alleviated.

Figure 4-24. Jennifer Higdon, *Ruminations*: "Where Everything Is Music," mm. 220–226
Music Copyright © 2016 by Jennifer Higdon [ASCAP].
Rumi texts translated by Coleman Barks and used with permission.

In direct music-poetic depiction, Rumi's text "Stop the words now" is immediately followed by two beats of silence (Figure 4-25a). Everything stops for a marked moment. In the next phrase, "Open the window in the center of your chest," the choir musically opens and ascends from F Lydian to G major. A striking event occurs in measures 234–235, as the a cappella choir floats in a higher tessitura for the text "let the spirits fly in and out." The harmony alternates between C major and F major for this effect of flying in and out. It ends on a polychordal allusion of G major with D minor (D^{13} if spelled vertically).

Figure 4-25a. Jennifer Higdon, *Ruminations*:
"Where Everything Is Music," mm. 230–235
Music Copyright © 2016 by Jennifer Higdon [ASCAP].
Rumi texts translated by Coleman Barks and used with permission.

The movement finishes with the words "Where Everything Is Music." Higdon prolongs the text by setting it three times, each in longer rhythms and each ending on an F major triad (Figure 4-25b). It is rare for a motive to be repeated three times within *Ruminations*, and Higdon's desire to imprint this text on the audience reveals its importance.

The melody starting in measure 230 beat three, shown in the piano reduction in Figure 4-25a, appears again in measure 247, seen below in Figure 4-25b, augmented in the vibraphone. This descending lyric motive, C–B–A–G–F, is threaded throughout *Ruminations*; it occurs also at the beginning of "All Day and Night," in measures 180–181 in the strings, in measures 212–213 (Figure 4-22) and 215 (Figure 4-23) in the strings and flute, and in measure 226 (Figure 4-24).

Figure 4-25b. Jennifer Higdon, *Ruminations*: "Where Everything Is Music," mm. 236–247
Music Copyright © 2016 by Jennifer Higdon [ASCAP].
Rumi texts translated by Coleman Barks and used with permission.

VI. Flowers Open Every Night (c. 2′30″)

Flowers open every night
across the sky, a breathing peace
and sudden flame catching.

Rumi, in translation by Coleman Barks

[reproduced with permission]

Each of the three solo movements adds one voice: from duet, to trio, to quartet. Each comes to have more unpredictable harmonies and melodies as well. Somewhat longer than the earlier solo movements, the sixth, an SATB quartet, is the most substantial on a number of levels. In the final measure of the previous movement, the orchestra modulates from a passage rooted on a D pedal to a tremolo E that crescendos severely into the sixth movement. Unpredictable and aurally unstable root movements occur in measures 257–261: B–A–E–D–C♯m–C–D–B♭-G♭ (Figure 4-26a). D♭ eventually becomes a prevailing harmony seen on cadence points in measures 262, 263, 266, and 268, though radical harmonic shifts continue throughout this section and throughout the movement.

Figure 4-26a. Jennifer Higdon, *Ruminations*:
"Flowers Open Every Night," mm. 253–263
Music Copyright © 2016 by Jennifer Higdon [ASCAP].
Rumi texts translated by Coleman Barks and used with permission.

Over measures 253–266, the soloists enter successively and repeat the text "Flowers open every night across the sky." Their imitation and rhythmic variation create the metaphor of flowers repeatedly opening. In measure 266, the voices build to a blossoming crescendo on the word "sky" (Figure 4-26b).

Figure 4-26b. Jennifer Higdon, *Ruminations*:
"Flowers Open Every Night," mm. 263–266
Music Copyright © 2016 by Jennifer Higdon [ASCAP].
Rumi texts translated by Coleman Barks and used with permission.

A harmonically unstable and unpredictable passage stretches from measure 268 to measure 272 over the text "and sudden flame catching. A breathing peace and sudden flame." The musical setting is rhythmically onomatopoetic. As seen in Figure 4-27, the word "catching" is accentuated with a rhythmic halt from the otherwise predominant eighth notes. "Sudden" in measure 270 is set in dotted rhythms. And "flame" in measure 272 is sung in flickering, wavering rhythms that are different in each voice.

Figure 4-27. Jennifer Higdon, *Ruminations*:
"Flowers Open Every Night," mm. 268–272
Music Copyright © 2016 by Jennifer Higdon [ASCAP].
Rumi texts translated by Coleman Barks and used with permission.

The movement's final measures create a picturesque image of delirium. The soloists sing in homophony but not in parallel motion, making this section even more dense. The harmonic roots change with every eighth note over measures 274–277, seen in Figure 4-28. While finally tonal, the result sounds anything but. On the final iteration of the word "catching" in measure 277, in subtle but effective word painting, the tenor changes pitch just a half beat before the other voices.

Harkening back to the opening of the piece, a trumpet solo announces the final movement. While at the beginning the trumpet's melody was a slow rising line, here it is presented in intense rhythmic diminution, with quintuplets then sextuplets propelling into the final movement. The trumpet's melody becomes associated with the concept of light: it initially appeared with the question "what was in that candle's light…?" and here it anticipates the opening line of the next poem, "In your light I learn how to love" (Figure 4-28).

Figure 4-28. Jennifer Higdon, *Ruminations*:
"Flowers Open Every Night," mm. 274–279
Music Copyright © 2016 by Jennifer Higdon [ASCAP].
Rumi texts translated by Coleman Barks and used with permission.

VII. In Your Light (c. 2′)

In your light I learn how to love.
In your beauty, how to make poems.

You dance inside my chest,
where no one sees you,

but sometimes I do,
and that sight becomes this art.

Rumi, in translation by Coleman Barks

[reproduced with permission]

In the final movement, the choir expands into divisi, texts are repeated, words are added, phrases arch, the tempo quickens, and the dynamics increase: everything intensifies. Rumi's poetry may be peaceful and contemplative, but Higdon's music brings out its euphoric and ecstatic characteristics.

The final movement launches out of the previous movement with a mere two beats of introduction after an exuberant trumpet solo (Figure 4-29). The choir enters on "In your light I learn how to love, In your beauty, how to make poems." The chorus moves in parallel, arching homophony. The work's unifying dotted-eighth and sixteenth rhythm is found on the words "how to" in measures 281 and 283 and on all instances of the word "poems."

The first words, "In your light," harken back to the central theme of the first movement. Rumi does not clarify to whom the poem is directed, to whom "your" refers—perhaps another soul, a deity, but clearly someone outside oneself. To portray the light, Higdon uses the key of C: in the first movement, the first chord on the word "light" was a clear reference to C Lydian (see Figure 4-1 to compare these two moments). Here it is a C major chord in the context of C Mixolydian.

Figure 4-29. Jennifer Higdon, *Ruminations*:
"Flowers Open Every Night," mm. 279–281
Music Copyright © 2016 by Jennifer Higdon [ASCAP].
Rumi texts translated by Coleman Barks and used with permission.

A one-measure bridge connects the first two lines of poetry. The orchestra plays in polyrhythms, with contrary motion that surges into the next choral phrase (Figure 4-30). This poetry now invokes dancing, "You dance inside my chest, where no one sees you." The contrapuntal juxtaposition of the female versus male voices represents this dancing. The tonality moves from C to A♭, then returns to C in the cadence on the last word of "where no one sees you." The choir holds the word "you" for three full beats, while the orchestra pushes forward.

Figure 4-30. Jennifer Higdon, *Ruminations*:
"Flowers Open Every Night," mm. 285–290
Music Copyright © 2016 by Jennifer Higdon [ASCAP].
Rumi texts translated by Coleman Barks and used with permission.

Over the next phrase, the choir sings "but sometimes I do, and that sight becomes this art." In a final repetition of the text, Higdon emphasizes

"In your light" by setting it in parallel motion framed in C major while arching to other chords that move in swift harmonic rhythm, changing on every eighth note. The choir rises to a peak on a C major triad on "sometimes I do" in measures 303–304 (Figure 4-31) as Higdon underscores this revelation and the value of truly being seen by the other.

Figure 4-31. Jennifer Higdon, *Ruminations*:
"Flowers Open Every Night," mm. 301–304
Music Copyright © 2016 by Jennifer Higdon [ASCAP].
Rumi texts translated by Coleman Barks and used with permission.

The ending is delirious, seemingly out of control, pressing toward a conclusion in a whirling dervish-like movement. The orchestra swirls through powerful, polyrhythmic runs involving sextuplets against eighth notes and sixteenth notes. The choir soars above the orchestra in parallel, homophonic arched contours in triads. Rather than giving the choir unpredictable harmonic densities and rapidly changing harmonic rhythms, Higdon lets the forward-moving phrases and the high tessitura of the unified chorus deliver an ultimate message: one of ecstasy found within the text.

The repetition of "and that sight becomes this art!" employs longer rhythms than the eighth notes that the chorus has mainly used to this point (Figure 4-32). Higdon also makes a subtle editorial splice within the poem: she borrows the phrase "this singing art" from movement six and inserts it here at the end of movement seven: "that sight becomes this singing art."

Figure 4-32. Jennifer Higdon, *Ruminations*:
"Flowers Open Every Night," mm. 307–313
Music Copyright © 2016 by Jennifer Higdon [ASCAP].
Rumi texts translated by Coleman Barks and used with permission.

Unlike many of Higdon's other compositions where the peak occurs somewhere around the last quarter of the work, the climax of *Ruminations* is saved for the last measure. The choir and orchestra arrive together and the perpetual motion finally releases on the word "art." Here "art" stands for the ultimate spiritual moment. It is a pure concept and therefore is set in C major. "This singing art" is a magnificent, spiritual, humanistic phrase, articulating a great mystery, the miracle of the human and spiritual connection, and the ensuing euphoria felt in such communion. It is beyond emotion, certainly beyond human understanding. The "singing art" is decidedly one of overwhelming joy, as Higdon has set it in the intellectual, emotional, and spiritual aspects of her composition.

CHAPTER FIVE

SOUTHERN GRACE

Southern Grace
(1998) 24 minutes
Solo quartet and SATB, SSAA, and TTBB chorus a cappella
Commissioned by the Philadelphia Singers, David Hayes, Music Director
With funds provided by the Musical Society of Philadelphia and
the John Simon Guggenheim Memorial Foundation
All texts in public domain, seven secular, one sacred

Pieces:

Fiddlin'
Wildwood Flower
Swing
My True Love's Hair
The Fox
The Riddle Song
Sourwood Mountain
Amazing Grace

Jennifer Higdon has written many small-form choral works that are equally worthy of attention as her large-form compositions. The small-form works are shorter than seven minutes and are performed a cappella or with a small chamber ensemble. *Southern Grace* is the only coordinated set of short choral songs in Higdon's oeuvre. On the score's cover she notes that, though the pieces were composed as a set, any movement may be performed separately. Each song is complete within itself, though a continuity runs through all of them. As Higdon might say, each uniquely conveys a poetic message and draws us deeply into the text.

Higdon's short-form works in general offer sophisticated challenges for directors and performers. Even when the pieces appear simple, challenges lie in the changing harmonies and meters and motivic developments through layers of added tones and counterpoint. These difficulties will be discovered in rehearsal, but when performed well, they may sound easy to accomplish.

Southern Grace is a collection of eight songs that suggest musical styles indigenous to the southern United States. Higdon grew up in the South and has an innate understanding of the styles and contexts of its music. She writes:

> I was born in Brooklyn, New York, but having grown up in Georgia and Tennessee, I feel my roots are mostly Southern. My family lived in Atlanta until I was ten, and then my parents decided that my brother and I should be closer to our grandparents. My parents bought a farm in a tiny place called Seymour, Tennessee, which was geographically situated between our two sets of grandparents. I lived in Seymour until I was eighteen and then moved away to college. Although being from the South can be emotionally complicated, I know that my musical aesthetic was deeply influenced by the land, sounds, people, and music of my Southern upbringing.

Higdon has provided the following background for *Southern Grace* in the program notes on her website:

> *Southern Grace* is my version of many of the Southern tunes that are popular in the Appalachian region. Each movement has been rewritten in a different manner: often, only the words of the original tune remain; sometimes a fragment of the melody remains but everything around it has been recomposed. One of the movements, "Fiddlin'," is an original work that reflects a musical genre of the region. Though these songs have been rewritten, the color and flavoring are still there: homegrown from a Southern upbringing.

I. Fiddlin'

SATB (3'19"), secular

"Fiddlin'" is set in a Southern Harmony style.[1] The text is entirely assigned to solfège syllables, in a Southern folk, fiddle approximation. The voices become instrument-like, imitating fiddles of various shapes and sizes arranged in interweaving musical lines, in a direct relationship to the title. The work offers a fun way for choirs to work on solfège. It is energetic, challenging, and enjoyable to rehearse and perform.

---

[1] The Southern Harmony style of singing is rooted in the American colonial era, "when singing schools convened to provide instruction in choral singing, especially for use in church services. ... Its distinguishing feature was the use of four separate shapes that indicated the notes according to the rules of solfège" ("*Southern Harmony*," *Wikipedia*). One such compilation was *The Southern Harmony, and Musical Companion* by William Walker, pub. 1835.

The song is in traditional song form, A-A'-B-A", with the opening section in C major. The altos begin on a rhythmic drone on C, adding occasional grace notes before the beat, or acciaccaturas, which are a common ornament in fiddle music (see Figure 5-1). The drone creates a foundation for the pentatonic melody sung by the sopranos and tenors in measure 5.

Figure 5-1. Jennifer Higdon, *Southern Grace*: "Fiddlin'," mm. 3–7
Music Copyright © 1998 by Jennifer Higdon [ASCAP].

The A' section begins in measure 13, where the entrances are in stretto one beat apart. Variation and counterpoint increase until the one-measure bridge in measure 21, where the meter shifts to 3/4 and the voices sing together on a repeated rhythm of an eighth note plus two sixteenths, which is a common rhythm in fiddle music (Figure 5-2). This pattern is voiced on open fourths and fifths, which are the easiest and most common intervals for double stops in fiddle music. In measure 22, the B section begins. The basses take on the role of an upright bass and play only on the main beats of the 4/4 meter. Occasional grace notes continue to be used, and the three upper voices incorporate parallel thirds.

Figure 5-2. Jennifer Higdon, *Southern Grace*: "Fiddlin'," mm. 21–24
Music Copyright © 1998 by Jennifer Higdon [ASCAP].

The composition becomes wild and unpredictable as it evolves into a raucous barn dance. Broken, irregular rhythms are exchanged between all four parts and combine to outline the pentatonic melody, but the absence of a repetitive fiddler-style ostinato leaves listeners without a foundation. Complexity is increased by the scattered and fragmented entrances in measures 32–35 (Figure 5-3). The rhythms quicken from eighth notes to sixteenth notes, and the contrapuntal activity builds to a peak in measure 45, which arrives on a key change to B♭ major (Figure 5-4). The dance has heated up.

Figure 5-3. Jennifer Higdon, *Southern Grace*: "Fiddlin'," mm. 32–35
Music Copyright © 1998 by Jennifer Higdon [ASCAP].

Figure 5-4. Jennifer Higdon, *Southern Grace*: "Fiddlin'," mm. 42–45
Music Copyright © 1998 by Jennifer Higdon [ASCAP].

A peak in measure 45 lasts just one measure. It is followed by a contrasting subito *p* lyric theme. The sopranos and basses sing an imitative variation of the theme from measure 22 (Figure 5-2), now in eighth notes (Figure 5-5).

Figure 5-5. Jennifer Higdon, *Southern Grace*: "Fiddlin'," mm. 45–47
Music Copyright © 1998 by Jennifer Higdon [ASCAP].

Continuing in B♭ major, the opening theme, slightly altered in the soprano line, returns in measure 54 as the A" in the A-A'-B-A" structure. The inner voices ascend in parallel thirds. Figure 5-6 shows the climactic race to the finish. The voices build to *ff*, which arrives on open fourths with a fermata to complete the ecstatic dance.

Other than solfège, there is no text in "Fiddlin'," but there is a music–text relationship in that solfège is performed on techniques borrowed from fiddle music. "Fiddlin'" shows that solfège, though challenging, can be fun and rewarding.

Figure 5-6. Jennifer Higdon, *Southern Grace*: "Fiddlin'," mm. 63–66
Music Copyright © 1998 by Jennifer Higdon [ASCAP].

II. Wildwood Flower

Solo SATB quartet with SATB chorus (3'36"), secular

I'll twine with my ring, made of raven black hair,
A rose so red, and lily so fair, the myrtle so green,
With its emerald hue, and pale ermeta, with eyes of dark blue,
He taught me to love him, he called me his flow'r,
A blossom to cheer him, through life's weary hour;
I'll wake from my dream, for my idol is clay,
My passion for loving him has vanished away,
He taught me to love him, he promised me to love,
To cherish me always all others above,
Another has won him I'm sorry to tell,
He left me no warning no words of farewell,
I'll dance and sing my life shall be gay,
I'll stop this wild weeping and drive my sorrow away,
I'll live yet to see him make right that dark hour when he neglected his
frail wildwood flow'r.

"Wildwood Flower" is a variant of the song "I'll Twine 'Mid the Ringlets," published in 1860 by composer Joseph Philbrick Webster, with lyrics attributed to Maud Irving.

"Wildwood Flower," a folk song with a nineteenth-century text, features a solo quartet that alternates in call-and-response with an SATB chorus. The piece is strophic; for the first half the solo quartet sings a verse, followed by the chorus; halfway through, the pattern is reversed and the chorus offers a verse followed by the quartet. The overall structure is as follows:

Quartet, 8 bars
Chorus response, 8 bars
Quartet, 8 bars
Chorus response, 8 bars
Chorus, 8 bars
Quartet response, 8 bars
Chorus coda, 8 bars

The song tells of the loss of love, lessons learned, and thoughts of redemption. The work's most apparent text painting is the use of E♭ major in the opening solo sections, which speak of love and hope, set against the relative key of C minor in the choral responses, which imply that this love will be unrequited. See Figure 5-7.

The first two quartet sections are in 4/4 meter, followed by choral sections in 2/4 meter. This truncated meter brings increased motion and contrapuntal interest in the inner voices. The choral responses are higher in tessitura with wider intervallic leaps than in the solo quartet. In the quartet, the outer voices, soprano and bass, are coupled against the inner voices as a prevailing texture.

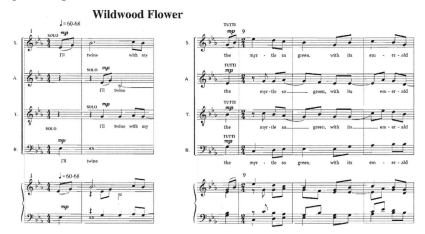

Figure 5-7. Jennifer Higdon, *Southern Grace*:
"Wildwood Flower," pickups to mm. 1–2 and 9–11
Music Copyright © 1998 by Jennifer Higdon [ASCAP].
Text in public domain.

The solo quartet and chorus exchange functions at the song's midpoint, measure 33, at the text "He taught me to love him, he promised me to love, to cherish me always all others above." The chorus echoes the speaker's emotions rather than performing their usual function of commenting on them. They join in the speaker's personal sorrow and express her sustained hope for the lover's affection. The tessitura remains relatively high throughout, and the ascent to a high point in measure 37, seen in Figure 5-8, underscores her intense emotion. As her broken heart is revealed, the chorus peaks on an Eb chord. The melody descends on the text "another has won him I'm sorry to tell, he left me no warning, no words of farewell." Dejection and hopelessness are felt in this falling cadence.

Figure 5-8. Jennifer Higdon, *Southern Grace*: "Wildwood Flower," mm. 33–40
Music Copyright © 1998 by Jennifer Higdon [ASCAP].
Text in public domain.

The quartet responds in soprano–bass and alto–tenor duets. The speaker promises that she will not spend her days in mourning: "I'll dance and I'll sing and my life shall be gay, I'll stop this wild weeping and drive my sorrow away." Higdon returns to the opening lilting themes as the young lady expresses her resolve to make the best of things.

In the coda, which begins in measure 49, the chorus assumes the same duet configuration as the soloists and offers a moral to the story. The coda begins with a return to the mourning key of C minor, but as if in defiance, it concludes in E♭ major, the key aligned with the optimistic portions of the poem. The text is "I'll live yet to see him make right that dark hour, when he neglected his frail wildwood flow'r." The lady is resigned to her fate yet vows to help him see the error of his ways. As shown in Figure 5-9, the final measures reveal her resignation as the voices descend and resolve. The counterpoint ultimately comes to an end as the flower petals close.

Figure 5-9. Jennifer Higdon, *Southern Grace*: "Wildwood Flower," mm. 52–56
Music Copyright © 1998 by Jennifer Higdon [ASCAP].
Text in public domain.

Even if "Wildwood Flower" sounds like a simple folk tune, it represents an ill-fated love through creative voicings and harmonies. The dueling duets of SB versus AT represent the jilted woman's pain and struggle. The all-knowing choral narration, in mostly homochoral writing, comments in a role similar to a Greek chorus. These conditions change when the woman accepts her outcome, at which point the chorus uses contrapuntal textures that were previously set for the soloists.

III. Swing

SATB (1'40"–2'), secular

> *Way down low in the cedar swamp, waters deep and muddy,*
> *There I met a pretty little miss, there I kissed my honey.*
> *Swing a lady up and down, swing a lady home,*
> *Swing a lady up and down, swing a lady home.*
> *Built my love a big fine house, built it in the garden,*
> *Put her in and she jumped out, fare you well my darling,*
> *Swing a lady up and down, swing a lady home,*
> *Swing a lady up and down, swing a lady home.*
> *Black-eyed girl is mad at me, blue-eyed girl won't have me,*
> *If I can't get the one I love, I guess I'll never marry.*
> *Swing a lady up and down, swing a lady low,*
> *Swing a lady up and down, swing a lady home.*
> *The older she gets the prettier she gets, I tell you she's my honey,*
> *makes me work all through the week and get stove wood on Sunday.*
> *Swing a lady up and down, swing a lady home.*
> *Way down low in the cedar swamp, waters deep and muddy,*
> *There I met a pretty little miss, there I kissed my honey.*

To this point, *Southern Grace* has contained a fiddle tune and a somber folk song. The next song, "Swing," is an Appalachian-style up-tempo dance tune. It is in D major, a good key for country dance instruments such as fiddle, banjo, guitar, and bass. The male voices are featured and court the female voices, which, though reticent at first, gradually become more involved. The speaker of the poem is a line dance caller, who calls directions for the dancers. He is represented by the male voices.

The song is structured in a loose verse and refrain form. The verses and refrains are similar on each return but are varied to such an extent that the song is not strophic.

For the four-measure introduction, the tenors and basses repeat the word "swing" in overlapping alternations (see Figure 5-10). The line dance caller starts up in measure 4, where his first line hints that this is an outdoor dance: "Way down low in the cedar swamp, waters deep and muddy."

Swing

Figure 5-10. Jennifer Higdon, *Southern Grace*: "Swing," mm. 1–6
Music Copyright © 1998 by Jennifer Higdon [ASCAP].
Text in public domain.

After the men sing, "there I kissed my honey," they continue with the recurring chorus, "Swing a lady up and down, swing a lady home." The women join in the fun on the word "swing." See Figure 5-11.

Figure 5-11. Jennifer Higdon, *Southern Grace*: "Swing," mm. 14–17
Music Copyright © 1998 by Jennifer Higdon [ASCAP].
Text in public domain.

The next verse begins in measure 27 as a conversation between men. The basses sing "built my love a big fine house," and the tenors complete that thought, "built it in the garden." The basses continue, "put her in and she jumped out"; the tenors finish, "fare you well my darling." The women rejoin in the chorus in measure 34, again singing only the word "swing."

In a three-measure bridge to the next verse (measures 42–44), the men sustain the last word of the chorus. The score directs the women to clack their tongues on the roof of their mouths, in a teasing, taunting manner.

In the third verse, the men sing "black-eyed girl is mad at me," and the tenors emphasize the lady's displeasure by repeating "mad at me" in rhythmic diminution. They continue, "blue-eyed girl won't have me," and in despair, the basses repeat that phrase. See Figure 5-12.

Figure 5-12. Jennifer Higdon, *Southern Grace*: "Swing," mm. 45–50
Music Copyright © 1998 by Jennifer Higdon [ASCAP].
Text in public domain.

The male voices gather their energies on "if I can't get the one I love, I guess I'll never marry." Their descending line crescendos to *f*, communicating a kind of fear about the idea that they might never marry (Figure 5-13). The women continue clacking their tongues, remaining aloof while the courting men plead. In measure 55, the men cadence on an open fourth, as they do often in this piece. Their open fourths imply the common tuning intervals (sometimes inverted as fifths) for folk instruments, including guitar, banjo, and fiddle.

In the next chorus in measures 56–63, the women offer a hint of hope by becoming more involved in the dance. Their interjection "swing" is set in more frequent, crisp sixteenth notes. They sing on the beat initially, and then move to the offbeats and add more text, "up, down, low."

Figure 5-13. Jennifer Higdon, *Southern Grace*: "Swing," mm. 54–57
Music Copyright © 1998 by Jennifer Higdon [ASCAP].
Text in public domain.

The women end the chorus by singing firmly on the beat, "swing, swing, home." They are joining in the dance and giving in to the pleading of the men.

They still play coy, however, and return to offbeat tongue clacks in measure 64. The men, undaunted in their pursuit, again sing the folk tune: "The older she gets the prettier she gets, I tell you she's my honey, makes me work all through the week and get stove wood on Sunday." The first altos join for just the final eighth note of every other measure. These syllables they sing are "the," "my," "all," and "on," which do not create a meaningful phrase, but do create anticipation.

On the next chorus in measure 72, at long last, all four voices join in the dance. This is the only homophony in this piece; it gathers energy as the ending approaches.

The final verse begins in measure 76, where the sopranos sing a descending unison melody with the men, while the altos repeat the word "low" in an offbeat ostinato on a low D (Figure 5-14). These effects paint the text "way down low." All parts converge on the word "swing" in measure 84, the men on the beat and the women responding in syncopation. The dance winds down in diminuendo, before the choir strikes a *subito ff* on the last "swing." Everyone clacks their tongues exultantly on the final offbeat.

Figure 5-14. Jennifer Higdon, *Southern Grace*: "Swing," mm. 76–77 and 86–91
Music Copyright © 1998 by Jennifer Higdon [ASCAP].
Text in public domain.

IV. My True Love's Hair

SSAA (3'38"), secular

> *Black is the color of my true love's hair*
> *His face is something wondrous and fair,*
> *The prettiest eyes and the neatest hands,*
> *I love the ground whereon he stands.*

> *I love my love and well he knows, I love the ground whereon he goes,*
> *If you on earth no more I see, I can't serve you as you have me,*
> *The winter's past and the leaves are green, the time is past that we have seen,*
> *But still I hope the time will come, when you and I shall be as one,*
> *My own true love, so fare you well, the time has come, but I wish you well,*
> *But still I hope, the time would come, when you and I shall be as one,*
> *I go to Clyde for to weep, but satisfied I never sleep*
> *I'll write to you a few lines, I'll suffer death ten thousand times.*

> *Black is the color of my true love's hair*
> *His face is something wondrous and fair,*
> *The prettiest eyes and the neatest hands,*
> *I love the ground whereon he stands.*

Alan Lomax, the late folklorist and musicologist, attributes "Black Is the Color of My True Love's Hair" to a nineteenth-century Scottish origin. The folk song made its way across the Atlantic, probably through Scottish immigrants, reaching North Carolina and Appalachia. In the original text, the line "I go to the Clyde to mourn and weep" refers to the River Clyde in Scotland. The song was first collected by the English folk-music archivist Cecil Sharp, who notated and recorded it during a 1916 trip to North Carolina. He then published it in 1917 in his *English Folk Songs of the Southern Appalachians*.

Higdon has kept the original text but composed new music. "My True Love's Hair" is a gentle love song told from a female perspective. Accordingly, Higdon set it for women's voices.

The poem's speaker is a young lady smitten by love. Her heart's palpitations are heard in the many harmonic seconds that appear throughout the work. In the first line, seconds occur on the following italicized words: "Black is the color *of my* true *love's hair*, his *face is something wondrous and fair*." They complicate what could otherwise be a simple harmonic fabric. The first four measures are also complicated by changing meters, which are used here for text scansion and are otherwise relatively rare in

Southern Grace. The meter is 4/4 for two measures, 3/4, 5/4, and 4/4 again, as seen below in Figure 5-15a.

The key begins in F Lydian. The melody rises and falls, like sighs from someone in love. It rises for "of my true" and "his face is something wondrous," and falls on "and the neatest hands," as the speaker looks down at her love's hands (Figure 5-15b). On "the ground whereon he stands," the gaze and melody further descend.

Figure 5-15a. Jennifer Higdon, *Southern Grace*: "My True Love's Hair," mm. 1–4
Music Copyright © 1998 by Jennifer Higdon [ASCAP].
Text in public domain.

Figure 5-15b. Jennifer Higdon, *Southern Grace*: "My True Love's Hair," mm. 6–8
Music Copyright © 1998 by Jennifer Higdon [ASCAP].
Text in public domain.

Beginning in measure 8, the divided sopranos imitate each other in descending passages on the text "I love my love and well he knows." The imitative counterpoint expands into a three-voice stretto with entrances one beat apart as her passion intensifies on the repeat of "I love the ground whereon he goes." The lines continue to cascade for "if you on earth no more I see, I can't serve you as you have me" (Figure 5-16); the descent depicts both the earth and her resignation. The music arrives not on a triad but an F[6] chord, whose very voicing, an open fourth with a stacked second, reveals her barren emotional state. This is set on a fermata in measure 14.

Figure 5-16. Jennifer Higdon, *Southern Grace*:
"My True Love's Hair," mm. 12–14
Music Copyright © 1998 by Jennifer Higdon [ASCAP].
Text in public domain.

The young woman seems ready to move forward as she sings, "The winter's past and the leaves are green, the time is past that we have seen." Though her words imply she may be ready to put this love behind her, the music reveals her true feelings. The phrase begins on a B diminished triad, an unstable harmony, and a string of ungrounded seconds follows. Starting in the pickup to measure 19, the texture is homorhythmic except that running eighth notes in the lower altos evoke an underlying restlessness (Figure 5-17). The soprano melody rises in expression of her hope, "but still I hope the time will come, when you and I shall be as one."

Figure 5-17. Jennifer Higdon, *Southern Grace*:
"My True Love's Hair," pickup to mm. 19–22
Music Copyright © 1998 by Jennifer Higdon [ASCAP].
Text in public domain.

In measure 23, the voices converge as the woman seems to be letting go of her love: "My own true love, so fare you well" (Figure 5-18). Then the three lower voices rise to express her renewed yearning: "but still I hope, the time would come, when you and I shall be as one." The depth of her longing is depicted as the second altos drop to a low G in measure 29 just before the first sopranos climb to a high G in measure 30. A unique moment in Higdon's music occurs here. Instead of the counterpoint giving way to homophony as is most common when Higdon approaches a peak, the voices separate and cascade in imitative scales, from the highest voice to the lowest. In an instance of musical irony the voices become independent, since they are not "as one."

Figure 5-18. Jennifer Higdon, *Southern Grace*:
"My True Love's Hair," mm. 23–32
Music Copyright © 1998 by Jennifer Higdon [ASCAP].
Text in public domain.

The sopranos and altos mourn in descending lines, "I go to Clyde for to weep." The ensuing text, in C Lydian, is "but satisfied I never sleep." Imitative stretto portrays the sleepless state of unrequited love.

The imitative counterpoint continues to reveal the woman's angst for her would-be lover: "I'll write you a few lines, I'll suffer death ten thousand times." The falling phrases hint that this death is very deep indeed. The key shifts from C Lydian to A minor. As the cadence in measure 38 is approached with retardations and suspensions, it seems the young woman would delay this acceptance. The bitter conclusion is reached on stacked seconds, A–B–C–D. See Figure 5-19.

Figure 5-19. Jennifer Higdon, *Southern Grace*:
"My True Love's Hair," mm. 37–38
Music Copyright © 1998 by Jennifer Higdon [ASCAP].
Text in public domain.

As usual, Higdon frames the work by bringing back the opening materials with subtle changes. F Lydian and changing meters return in measure 39. Seconds are again prevalent, sung in the sighing phrases of someone pining for love.

In the final words, "I love the ground whereon he stands," the first altos hold a suspension on the word "stands" (Figure 5-20). The lady is reluctant to give up hope; she prolongs her acceptance one beat longer. A fermata on their fourth beat further delays the final G triad. But in the context of F Lydian, this triad as well feels uneasy and not yet resolved. The woman's longing is still palpable even in the final measures.

Figure 5-20. Jennifer Higdon, *Southern Grace*:
"My True Love's Hair," pickup to mm. 45–46
Music Copyright © 1998 by Jennifer Higdon [ASCAP].
Text in public domain.

V. The Fox

SATB divisi (1'42"), secular

> *The fox started out one moonshiny night, he prayed for the Lord to give him light,*
> *For he had a mile to go that night before he reached his den-e-o,*
> *He came at last to the farmer's yard, where the ducks and chickens were plenty,*
> *Oh one of you will grease my beard, I'll take you to my den-e-o,*
> *He grabbed an old black duck by the neck and he threw her across his shoulder,*
> *The old black duck said "Quack! Quack!" and its long legs hung down-e-o.*
>
> *Quack! Quack! Quack! Old Granny Slipper Slopper jumped out of her bed,*
> *And out the window poked her grey head,*
> *"John, John, the black duck's gone with the fox straight to his den-e-o."*
> *Johnny Slipper Slopper jumped out of bed, he fell against the table and bumped his head,*
> *He fell over the cradle and thought he was dead and the fox got to his den-e-o.*
> *Slipper Slopper ran to the top of the hill, and he blew his horn so loud and shrill,*
> *But the fox got the best of the music still, safe home inside his den-e-o.*

"The Fox" is a Middle English poem from the fifteenth century, which Higdon has set to original vocals in the style of an Appalachian hills band. Marked *fast and spirited*, the voices sing nonsense syllables such as "ba-du" and "do-do-do" over the three-measure introduction (Figure 5-21). The intervals of fourths and fifths recall hunting horns, as the fox's pursuit of his prey is underway. Quickening rhythms, marked by acciaccaturas, represent his quickening pace: half notes give way to quarter notes, which then change to syncopated quarter notes and later eighth notes. The basses provide rhythmic grounding on the main beats.

Soloists narrate the story and play its characters. In the pickup to measure 4, the tenor soloist sings a pentatonic melody that leaps by fourths and fifths around G, consistent with the tuning notes of a banjo. The story begins, "The fox started out one moonshiny night, he prayed for the Lord to give him light, for he had a mile to go before he reached his den-e-o." The soloist's rhythm of one eighth and two sixteenth notes, which occurs often in this song, portrays the fox's running feet. See Figure 5-21.

The Fox

Figure 5-21. Jennifer Higdon, *Southern Grace*: "The Fox," mm. 1–4
Music Copyright © 1998 by Jennifer Higdon [ASCAP].
Text in public domain.

The acciaccaturas from the introduction, which ceased as the text began, return in measures 8–9, now on the offbeats (Figure 5-22). The meter changes from the opening 4/4 to 3/4 in measures 9 and 10, which compresses the rhythmic drive. A glissando in measure 10 zips up from F to G and brings a return to 4/4 meter in measure 11 for the next phrase of the soloist's text.

Figure 5-22. Jennifer Higdon, *Southern Grace*: "The Fox," mm. 8–11
Music Copyright © 1998 by Jennifer Higdon [ASCAP].
Text in public domain.

The baritone soloist now narrates in a new descending pentatonic tune, "He came at last to the farmer's yard, where the ducks and the chickens were plenty." As the baritone transforms to play the role of the fox, his voice becomes sinister in a lower tessitura: "Oh, one of you will grease my beard, I'll take you to my den-e-o." He sings alone for several measures, which create suspense. The other voices shout "ha, ha" on gleeful, unpitched exclamations (Figure 5-23).

Figure 5-23. Jennifer Higdon, *Southern Grace*: "The Fox," mm. 15–17
Music Copyright © 1998 by Jennifer Higdon [ASCAP].
Text in public domain.

As seen above in Figure 5-23, an alto soloist continues the story: "He grabbed an old black duck by the neck, and he threw her across his shoulder, the old black duck said, 'Quack! Quack!' And its long legs hung down-e-o." The basses and altos accompany her on droning open fourths and fifths. On the repeat of the phrase "and its long legs hung down-e-o," the soloist slides downward on a glissando that exaggerates the duck's hanging legs.

Meter continues to be a factor that underscores the story. In measure 22, it shifts to 5/4, giving room for three "Quacks!" which the altos cry out on unpitched offbeats (Figure 5-24). The metric expansion creates a dramatic pause on beat 4, as the duck is caught and the chase is briefly halted. Beat 5 contains the pickup note for the next verse in 4/4 time.

Figure 5-24. Jennifer Higdon, *Southern Grace*: "The Fox," mm. 21–23
Music Copyright © 1998 by Jennifer Higdon [ASCAP].
Text in public domain.

    A new saga begins as Granny Slopper is awakened by the ruckus. The upper voices, on a lyric melody contrasting with the rest of the song, describe Granny's action: "Old Granny Slipper Slopper jumped out of her bed, and out the window poked her grey head." The open fourths and fifths have ceased, as have the instrumental folk rhythms and nonsense syllables. In homophony on elongated note values of quarter and half notes, the sleepy melody is sung in *subito p*. See Figure 5-25.

Figure 5-25. Jennifer Higdon, *Southern Grace*: "The Fox," pickup to mm. 22–27
Music Copyright © 1998 by Jennifer Higdon [ASCAP].
Text in public domain.

As Granny realizes what has happened, her music changes dramatically. The soprano soloist calls for Grandad on a line that starts on shrill high Gs: "John, John, the black duck's gone, with the fox straight into his den-e-o." In alarm, Granny and the choir repeat "den-e-o" on quick rhythms, portraying the fox on the move again. See measures 31–32 in Figure 5-26.

Figure 5-26. Jennifer Higdon, *Southern Grace*: "The Fox," mm. 29–32
Music Copyright © 1998 by Jennifer Higdon [ASCAP].
Text in public domain.

Grandad jumps into action but only with some trouble. The tenor soloist narrates as Old Johnny Slipper Slopper jumps out of bed and trips over furniture, giving the fox time to get away. All the while as Grandad is trying to get up and save his duck, the sopranos and altos overlap on their repeats of the word "den-e-o."

The suspense builds as more and more sixteenth- and eighth-note patterns appear (seen in Figure 5-27). The chorus narrates as Old Slipper Slopper runs to the top of the hill and blows his hunting horn. They imitate the sound of the horn in measures 40–41 as an open fifth on G and D for the women is set over an open fifth of F and C for the men. The piled open fifths create a discordant polychord, sung on the horn-like syllables "bah-bah" in rising imitative counterpoint.

Figure 5-27. Jennifer Higdon, *Southern Grace*: "The Fox," mm. 35–40
Music Copyright © 1998 by Jennifer Higdon [ASCAP].
Text in public domain.

On the piece's characteristic eighth and two sixteenths rhythm, the narration continues: "But the fox got the best of the music still." The phrase ascends on a crescendo to a *f* on a D major triad, and a fermata causes the singers to pause on the word "still" in measure 42 of Figure 5-28. The chorus descends on the text "safe home inside his den-e-o." The basses, who had been silent during the fox's victory lap, join in the last two measures with the rest of the chorus and move in chromatic parallel fourths and fifths. A final "ha ha" expresses the fox's triumphal hurrah—both the song and the duck have reached their end.

Figure 5-28. Jennifer Higdon, *Southern Grace*: "The Fox," pickup to mm. 42–47
Music Copyright © 1998 by Jennifer Higdon [ASCAP].
Text in public domain.

VI. Riddle Song

SATB divisi (2'48"), secular

> *I gave my love a cherry that had no stone*
> *I gave my love a chicken that had no bones*
> *I gave my love a ring that had no end*
> *I gave my love a baby with no cryin'*
>
> *How can there be a cherry with no stone?*
> *How can there be a chicken with no bones?*
> *How can there be a ring that has no end?*
> *How can there be a baby with no cryin'?*
>
> *A cherry when it's bloomin' it has no stone*
> *A chicken when it's pippin' it has no bones*
> *A ring when it's rollin' it has no end*
> *A baby when it's sleepin' has no cryin'*

"Riddle Song" is a setting of a traditional folk song text, "I Gave My Love a Cherry." The poem has three verses. The first makes four statements, laying out four riddles. The second asks a question of each riddle, and the third solves them. Higdon makes this the musical structure. The song lies somewhere between an arrangement and an entirely new composition, as Higdon integrates her original music with portions of a traditional folk tune. For example, the first two measures reflect the original folk song, but measures 3–5 contain Higdon's original melody. The folk tune is quoted only in small pieces at the beginning and appears in almost a complete statement at the end of the piece.

Set for eight-part chorus in a slow tempo, the song opens with a lyric tenor solo. He serenely sings fragments of the folk song, supported harmonically by the three lower men's voices. They move in half notes in a bagpipe-like drone on an open, neutral syllable "ah." An antiphonal chorus texture begins as the women's voices alternate with the men's in call and response. The women's initial response to the solo loosely echoes the text in descant-style. The altos delay their entrance by an eighth note and delicately enhance the soprano's response to the tenor. See Figure 5-29.

Riddle Song

Figure 5-29. Jennifer Higdon, *Southern Grace*: "Riddle Song," pickup to mm. 1–6
Music Copyright © 1998 by Jennifer Higdon [ASCAP].
Text in public domain.

In the second verse the riddles emerge: "How can there be a cherry with no stone?" "How can there be a chicken with no bones?" "How can there be a ring that has no end?" and "How can there be a baby with no cryin'?" These four questions are asked by the sopranos, altos, and tenors. They sing in complex imitative counterpoint that bears no resemblance to the original folk tune. For each riddle, the voicing order is similar: as the phrase descends, the first sopranos begin, followed by first altos and tenors, and as the phrase turns upward, the second altos and second sopranos are added. See Figure 5-30. Open fifths in the basses provide harmonic grounding and a link to the texture of the first verse. They begin low for each question and then ascend, offering the effect of raising the question in the riddle.

Figure 5-30. Jennifer Higdon, *Southern Grace*: "Riddle Song," mm. 13–16
Music Copyright © 1998 by Jennifer Higdon [ASCAP].
Text in public domain.

The last riddle, "How can there be a baby with no cryin'?" ends differently. While the basses continue their now familiar open fifths, the other voices descend onto a secundal chord. The mystery of a baby who does not cry is couched in thickened counterpoint and no resolution: a $C^{6/9}$ chord in suspension moves to a $C^{7/9}$ chord held by a fermata in measure 21 (Figure 5-31). The effect is not one of finality.

Figure 5-31. Jennifer Higdon, *Southern Grace*: "Riddle Song," mm. 19–21
Music Copyright © 1998 by Jennifer Higdon [ASCAP].
Text in public domain.

The final verse, which begins in measure 22, is initiated by the unison altos singing the original folk tune, which has not been heard since a fragment in measures 9–10. The melody is decorated with falling open fifths in the sopranos against the open fifths ostinato in the basses. The basses' accompaniment syllable has changed from "ah" to "ooo," changing the tone for the answers to the riddles. The folk tune is heard throughout this final verse, except in the final measure where Higdon leaves something to the audience's imagination.

The antiphonal chorus from the first verse has not been abandoned. The altos solve the first riddle, "A cherry when it's bloomin' it has no stone," and the tenors follow with a repeat of the altos' rhythm but not their melody. The antiphonal structure occurs for all four answers and provides a framing to the work.

The formula used in measure 21 (see Figure 5-31 above) has come to express uncertainty regarding the riddles. It appears again at the end of the third solution in measure 27: like "a ring when it's rollin' it has no end," the C^7 cadence with a fermata is also without resolution. Higdon also uses the 5/4 meter to suspend the answer and prevent a predictable phrase ending. See Figure 5-32.

Figure 5-32. Jennifer Higdon, *Southern Grace*:
"Riddle Song," pickup to mm. 26–29
Music Copyright © 1998 by Jennifer Higdon [ASCAP].
Text in public domain.

"Riddle Song" starts and ends in F major. It ends specifically on an F^6 chord. The sixth, D, becomes a prominent color in the final measure, moving from first sopranos to the altos and finally to the second sopranos. The 5/4 meter returns in the last measure to aid the written ritardando and delay the final chord. The harmony continues the effect of the riddles: mystery lingers in the air.

VII. Sourwood Mountain

TTBB (1'28"), secular

> *Hi ho diddle hi day*
> *Chickens a-crowin' on Sourwood Mountain*
> *Fiddle hi diddle day hi ho diddle I day*
> *Get your dog and we'll go hunting*
> *Hi ho diddle I day*
> *I gotta gal in the head of the hollow*
> *She won't come and I won't call her*
> *Hi ho diddle I day*
> *She sits up there with old Si Hall*
> *Me and Jim can't go a-tall*
> *Hi ho diddle I day*
> *One of these days and it won't be long*
> *I'll get that gal and home I'm gone*
> *Hi ho diddle hi day-hey diddle day*

"Sourwood Mountain" honors the Appalachian folk-style with Higdon's special recipe. There are several traditional renderings of this Southern mountain tune, but Higdon references none of them. Her composition is for four-part male chorus, with the character *Boisterously* indicated at the head of the score. The use of men's voices seems characteristic of what one might expect from an outdoor concert in the Southern hills.

The song opens on four of the tuning notes of a banjo, G–D–G–[B]–D. The basses deliver these pitches in an irregular rhythm on the syllables "doe, doe, doe," as if imitating a banjo player warming up. As soon as their rhythm is established, Higdon alters it in almost every measure with syncopations and unpredictable entrances. The second tenors join in measure 2 on traditional folk nonsense syllables, "diddle hi diddle day, hi ho hi hi diddle." Their melody is pentatonic and linear, but the meters, which alternate between 4/4 and 3/4, create shifting accents and surprising rhythms. See Figure 5-33.

Sourwood Mountain

Figure 5-33. Jennifer Higdon, *Southern Grace*: "Sourwood Mountain," mm. 1–4
Music Copyright © 1998 by Jennifer Higdon [ASCAP].
Text in public domain.

Measure 7 brings a new bass line: alternating eighth notes in open fifths, as a plucked string bass would play (Figure 5-34). The tenors' melody infuses country-folk flavor as they sing about feral "chickens a-crowin' on Sourwood Mountain." Throughout the song, the storyline is interspersed with brief one- or two-measure sections that act like instrumental bridges. These are performed on folky nonsense syllables.

Figure 5-34. Jennifer Higdon, *Southern Grace*: "Sourwood Mountain," mm. 7–9
Music Copyright © 1998 by Jennifer Higdon [ASCAP].
Text in public domain.

The song continues in this manner. In each line, the first tenor delivers a short phrase of the story, followed by a quasi-instrumental response interjected by the other voices, as seen below in Figure 5-35.

Figure 5-35. Jennifer Higdon, *Southern Grace*:
"Sourwood Mountain," mm. 12–15
Music Copyright © 1998 by Jennifer Higdon [ASCAP].
Text in public domain.

Until this point, the melodies have been pentatonic and set over the pitches G and D. In measure 23, the key modulates down a step, and the open fifths drop to F and C. The energy increases through greater rhythmic complexity and unpredictable, offbeat accents. The voices alternate their eighth-note rhythms in an excited conversation. Figure 5-36 shows this bridge section that leads into verse two.

Figure 5-36. Jennifer Higdon, *Southern Grace*:
"Sourwood Mountain," mm. 23–29
Music Copyright © 1998 by Jennifer Higdon [ASCAP].
Text in public domain.

    The first tenors return with the same rhythms used in the last couplet: "One of these days and it won't be long [*hi ho diddle*, etc.] I'll get that gal and home I'm gone." The basses, playing the role of bass fiddles, continue their alternating eighth-note ostinato. Convinced about getting the gal, the tenors repeat their text and communicate their excitement in an upward portamento in measure 34. The meter condenses from 4/4 to 3/4 for a confident final repetition of "I'll get that girl and home I'm gone."

    The counterpoint intensifies until the tenors sing "day" on each beat while basses respond with "doe" on the offbeats (measures 42–44 in Figure 5-37). In the penultimate measure, measure 45, the tenors sustain an open fifth on F and C. Imitating a fiddle, they again slide upward. The basses join on the final beats with a *ff* "hey diddle day!" as the band comes to an exhilarating finish.

Figure 5-37. Jennifer Higdon, *Southern Grace*:
"Sourwood Mountain," mm. 38–46
Music Copyright © 1998 by Jennifer Higdon [ASCAP].
Text in public domain.

VIII. Amazing Grace

Dedicated to Higdon's brother: "For my beloved Andrew Blue"

SATB or TTBB (6'25"), sacred

Amazing grace how sweet the sound
That saved a wretch like me
I once was lost but now I'm found
Was blind but now I see

'Twas grace that taught my heart to fear
and grace my fears relieved,
how precious did that grace appear,
the hour I first believed

Through many dangers, toils and snares,
I have already come,
'Tis grace that brought me save thus far,
And grace will lead me home

How sweet the name of Jesus sounds in a believer's ear
It soothes his sorrow
Heals his wounds
And drives away his fear

When we've been there ten thousand years,
Bright shining as the sun,
We've no less days to sing God's praise,
Than when we'd first begun

"Amazing Grace" is the only sacred piece in *Southern Grace*. It uses the text and melody of a hymn published in 1779. The lyrics were written in 1772 by the Anglican clergyman and former slave trader John Newton. Legend has it that on one trading trip, Newton's ship was caught in a hurricane; afraid for his life, Newton converted to Christianity and vowed to change his ways. He later wrote "Amazing Grace," which referred to his reformation by God's grace after his contributions to slavery. Due in part to this legend, the hymn became a favorite in the American South, especially among slaves, and it was used by preachers who evangelized in the South during the early nineteenth century. This backstory is a primary reason the hymn would appear in and inspire the overall title of *Southern Grace*.

The score specifies that "Amazing Grace" is arranged by Higdon, even though much of it is newly composed. The original hymn tune appears in full for the first and last verses, and is used only in fragments in between.

Higdon arranged the piece for SATB and later scored it also for TTBB.

With the quarter note at 52–60, an introductory ostinato begins with a rocking, waving motion like the waves of the sea. This motion occurs in a voice exchange between the altos and tenors, who combine to create arpeggios. They repeat the words "How sweet" and "the sound." The tenors sing on a perfect forth (G to C), which are the first two pitches of the original hymn.

An alto soloist begins the hymn melody and is woven into the fabric created by the altos and tenors, scored in overlapping ranges. The tenors deliver wide, intervallic leaps, traveling at times the distance of a tenth, yet their line is linear, soaring, floating. The solo becomes integrated into the fabric rather than emerging as a dominant voice. See Figure 5-38.

Figure 5-38. Jennifer Higdon, *Southern Grace*:
"Amazing Grace," pickup to mm. 9–13
Music Copyright © 1998 by Jennifer Higdon [ASCAP].
Text in public domain.

After the solo ends in measure 21, the two-voice ostinato continues in wafting lines that portray grace as beautiful and relational. The basses enter in measure 24, deepening the musical texture. The sopranos join last, in measure 26, with a descant-like melody on verse two that recalls the hymn and becomes central to the work (Figure 5-39).

To increase the intensity and conviction communicated in the work, the tempo quickens at structural points. From the starting quarter note at 52–60, it increases incrementally until the quarter note is 92–96 when the hymn comes back in measure 96. The first increase of tempo appears in measure 27 at the start of verse two.

Figure 5-39. Jennifer Higdon, *Southern Grace*: "Amazing Grace," mm. 23–27
Music Copyright © 1998 by Jennifer Higdon [ASCAP].
Text in public domain.

A fragment of the hymn tune returns on "my fears," in the pickup to measure 31 (Figure 5-40). The final note of the hymn, G, is found through an octave displacement from the soprano in measure 30 to the bass on the downbeat of measure 33. The second verse concludes in measure 42 on a plagal cadence of F to C, a IV–I harmonic movement found on the final "amen" of many church hymns.

Figure 5-40. Jennifer Higdon, *Southern Grace*: "Amazing Grace," mm. 30–33
Music Copyright © 1998 by Jennifer Higdon [ASCAP].
Text in public domain.

For verse three, beginning in measure 42, the texture changes considerably, from a four-part homophonic cadence to a more intimate two-part conversation. The tempo increases to 66–72. The tenors sing an augmented rhythm that represents the note values of the hymn, while the sopranos have a decorative countermelody in contrary motion. Their running, arched passages with eighth and quarter notes develop the text "many dangers, toils and snares."

Until measure 56 there are no further references to the original hymn. Instead, arched and winding phrases provide a comfortable setting for a text that describes eternal safety: "It is grace that brought me safe thus far, and grace will lead me home." The harmony, here and throughout the arrangement, is quasi-pandiatonic: each line uses the C major scale, without direct concern over the resulting chordal harmonies. The C major chord is passed through on the word "home" in measure 56 (Figure 5-41).

Figure 5-41. Jennifer Higdon, *Southern Grace*: "Amazing Grace," mm. 49–56
Music Copyright © 1998 by Jennifer Higdon [ASCAP].
Text in public domain.

The counterpoint becomes inverted in measure 56 as the tenors take over the sopranos' descant-like melody, while the altos inherit and alter the tenors' previous melody. In measure 58, the altos take up and the sopranos resume the descant, which is now present in all three upper voices. The basses thicken the fabric with their deep voices and descending line, "I have already traveled safe thus far." Their entrance corresponds with the concept of traveling as it winds downward. The basses then rise a full octave as they rejoice at having "traveled safe thus far." See Figure 5-42.

Figure 5-42. Jennifer Higdon, *Southern Grace*: "Amazing Grace," mm. 58–61
Music Copyright © 1998 by Jennifer Higdon [ASCAP].
Text in public domain.

The choir's final repetition of "grace will lead me home" contains a particularly cogent example of text painting. The word "home" is buried in the inner voices, while the sopranos and basses do not sing it at all. Rather than singing "home," the basses sing "how" in measure 63, which begins the next phrase, "how sweet." A cadence was expected, but not given. The singers are not home yet.

In the next section of text, the choir sings, "How sweet the name of Jesus sounds in a believer's ear, it soothes his sorrow, heals his wounds and drives away his fear." It starts unexpectedly as the time signature changes from the previous 4/4 to 2/4 meter in measure 63 and to 3/4 meter in measure 64 (Figure 5-43). The effect broadens the music. The basses strike sustained tones on various unpredictable beats while, over measures 63–68, the original hymn melody is exchanged among the altos, sopranos, and tenors in near homophony. In Figure 5-43, these notes are marked with boxes. The text is interrupted with rests that create irregular rhythmic accents.

Figure 5-43. Jennifer Higdon, *Southern Grace*: "Amazing Grace," mm. 63–68
Music Copyright © 1998 by Jennifer Higdon [ASCAP].
Text in public domain.

In the fifth verse, the bass and alto voices return to decorative motivic lines heard earlier in the composition: "When we've been there ten thousand years, bright shining as the sun, we've no less days to sing God's praise, than when we'd first begun" (Figure 5-44). Eternity and a sense of timelessness are immediate in the weaving vocal parts, underscored in the deeper vocal sonorities and continuous animated counterpoint.

Figure 5-44. Jennifer Higdon, *Southern Grace*: "Amazing Grace," mm. 80–86
Music Copyright © 1998 by Jennifer Higdon [ASCAP].
Text in public domain.

The tenors and sopranos, meanwhile, have slower rhythms that hint at the rhythm of the original hymn tune. A small portion of the hymn melody is hidden in the soprano line in measures 92–94, where the downbeats of each measure are the last three notes of the hymn: E–D–C (see the notes in boxes in Figure 5-45). The harmony continues to be pandiatonic in C major.

Figure 5-45. Jennifer Higdon, *Southern Grace*: "Amazing Grace," mm. 91–94
Music Copyright © 1998 by Jennifer Higdon [ASCAP].
Text in public domain.

The final section begins with a climactic ascent to D major—a key used throughout Western classical music history to represent victorious, triumphal moments. The tempo increases to the fastest part of the work, and the sopranos repeat the first verse on the complete, original hymn tune. The tenors sing running eighth notes against the soprano melody. The basses and altos combine on grand, elongated chords, representative of the chords played by a church organ. See Figure 5-46.

Figure 5-46. Jennifer Higdon, *Southern Grace*:
"Amazing Grace," pickup to mm. 96–104
Music Copyright © 1998 by Jennifer Higdon [ASCAP].
Text in public domain.

In measure 119, the chorus gathers in *ff* homorhythm. They are forceful, almost like in one of George Frideric Handel's regal processions. The sopranos, singing on some of the highest notes of the work, create a moment that is dramatic yet angelic. See Figure 5-47.

Figure 5-47. Jennifer Higdon, *Southern Grace*: "Amazing Grace," mm. 119–125
Music Copyright © 1998 by Jennifer Higdon [ASCAP].
Text in public domain.

For the coda in measure 125, the phrases stretch out as the tempo slows to a quarter note at 72 and the meter broadens to 4/4 (seen in Figure 5-47 above). Fragments of the text "and grace will lead me home" are repeated in transparent counterpoint, providing a sense of peace. The soprano melody descends, the tenors intone on open fifths, and the altos resume the wavelike motion from the piece's beginning (Figure 5-48). This reprise conveys calm assurance of an eventual homecoming. All the lines have a breath mark with a fermata before the final word "home." After having taceted for 6 measures, the basses reenter on a low D.

As a whole, the work ascends by one whole step, beginning in C major and ending in D major. Grace is, in this regard, uplifting. Through winding counterpoint between voices, Higdon communicates that grace occurs in relationship with others.

Figure 5-48. Jennifer Higdon, *Southern Grace*: "Amazing Grace," mm. 129–132
Music Copyright © 1998 by Jennifer Higdon [ASCAP].
Text in public domain.

In Summation

The eight songs collected in *Southern Grace* are an homage to traditional music from Appalachia, inspired from local ballads, folk songs, dance and band music, and a hymn tune—music that Higdon has heard all her life. The overall mood of the set is light: the texts in "Fiddlin'," "Riddle Song," "Swing," and "The Fox" naturally demand less serious settings than the poetry by Rumi and John Donne, for example. And the romantic ballads "Wildwood Flower" and "My True Love's Hair," though not light music, are more intimate and personal than many of Higdon's other works. This contrast demonstrates that Higdon's innate ability and artistic instincts can shine through in all her compositions; she is not locked into a certain voicing, instrumentation, or level of gravity in which to communicate her compositional style. Regardless of a work's size or scope, her commitment to convey the text in music remains consistent, and she seems to have unlimited creativity to combine musical elements to enhance the text's meaning.

Chapter Six

Invitation to Love

Invitation to Love
(2016) 4.5 minutes
SATB, a cappella
Commissioned by Chorus America in honor of Ann Meier Baker,
Director of Chorus America, appointed in 2015
Poem by Paul Laurence Dunbar, secular

> *Come when the nights are bright with stars*
> *Or come when the moon is mellow;*
> *Come when the sun his golden bars*
> *Drops on the hayfield yellow.*
> *Come in the twilight soft and gray,*
> *Come in the night or come in the day,*
> *Come, O love, whene'er you may,*
> *And you are welcome, welcome.*
>
> *You are sweet, O Love, dear Love,*
> *You are soft as the nesting dove.*
> *Come to my heart and bring it to rest*
> *As the bird flies home to its welcome nest.*
>
> *Come when my heart is full of grief*
> *Or when my heart is merry;*
> *Come with the falling of the leaf*
> *Or with the redd'ning cherry.*
> *Come when the year's first blossom blows,*
> *Come when the summer gleams and glows,*
> *Come with the winter's drifting snows,*
> *And you are welcome, welcome.*

Invitation to Love premiered in June 2016 at the Chorus America Conference held in Cincinnati, Ohio. It was beautifully presented by the Vocal Arts Ensemble of Cincinnati with Craig Hella Johnson conducting. The piece spoke to the rather sophisticated audience, who showed their deep appreciation in a lengthy standing ovation and enthusiastic comments afterward. I was present and found it to be a penetrating and deeply moving work. I have performed it numerous times since then, and in each performance, on tour and at home, audiences consistently appreciate the music and its message.

The tempo is slow, at a quarter note equals 56–60 beats per minute. The opening text is an invitation: "Come when the nights are bright with stars Or come when the moon is mellow." The music begins simply, in a low tessitura with C major triads (Figure 6-1a). The phrase arches up then down and then makes two more small arches, like breathing: inhaling and exhaling, almost in a sigh.

Figure 6-1a. Jennifer Higdon, *Invitation to Love*, mm. 1–6
Music Copyright © 2016 by Jennifer Higdon [ASCAP].
Text by Paul Laurence Dunbar.

Higdon relies heavily on pandiatonicism for this work; the pitches remain within a scale without necessarily creating functional chords. Freely moving across the C major scale, the harmonies are lush and extraordinarily colorful. Added seconds color key words, such as "when the sun" in measures 7–8 (Figure 6-1b), or they appear near the ends of phrases, such as on "mellow" in the first phrase and "yellow" in the second. But phrases also often reach relatively pure conclusions: on a triad, for example.

New sections of text often begin with unprepared harmonies. These are either a large interval away from, or only distantly related to, the preceding chord. For example, at the second invitation, which comes in measure 7, "Come when the sun his golden bars Drops on the hayfield yellow," the sopranos leap a perfect fourth higher than the last note of the previous phrase. The phrase start is accentuated with *mf* subito decrescendo. Stacked thirds with chordal extensions dominate the harmony. The melody arches slightly, rising for the word "hayfield" and imitating its movement of waving in the wind. The melody then descends to trace the drop of the sun's rays. This five-measure phrase cadences on a G major triad with no added tones. The G major triad becomes something of a home chord.

Figure 6-1b. Jennifer Higdon, *Invitation to Love*, mm. 7–11
Music Copyright © 2016 by Jennifer Higdon [ASCAP].
Text by Paul Laurence Dunbar.

In a burst of color, the choir changes from G major to an F major[11] sung significantly higher on the downbeat of measure 12 (Figure 6-2). The singers offer another invitation, "Come in the twilight soft and gray, Come in the night or come in the day." While the harmonies are dense with added seconds, all pitches come from C major.

Figure 6-2. Jennifer Higdon, *Invitation to Love*, mm. 12–13 and 16–17
Music Copyright © 2016 by Jennifer Higdon [ASCAP].
Text by Paul Laurence Dunbar.

"Come O love, whenever you may, And you are welcome," is the next invitation, and this one as well begins in a somewhat surprising fashion (Figure 6-3). A dynamic increase to *mf* marks the text, which the male voices sing substantially higher than in the preceding cadence: the top tenors and basses are each up a seventh. Sudden harmonic shifts and gender-specific writing become common in this work. What does this mean in terms of the text? Does love come to us in various forms, often surprising, without anticipation? Does it come in relationship to the other, and is this represented in the gender-specific voicings that Higdon uses? It is not a stretch to find evidence to substantiate those premises.

A conversation between male and female voices ensues. In measure 19, the sopranos sing a delicate, cascading plea, "Love, come, O love." The altos repeat the text in counterpoint, as the male voices urge love to come "whenever you may." The text expands to include and repeat "And you are welcome." The female voices ascend and then descend, urging love to come, assuring it that it is desired. The male voices too implore with insistence, "You are welcome." In ascending parallel chords with added tones, they accelerando and crescendo creating what feels like a departure from the C major tonal center. But all pitches are still from C major until measure 25, and the effect is caused by changing chord roots.

Figure 6-3. Jennifer Higdon, *Invitation to Love*, mm. 18–26
Music Copyright © 2016 by Jennifer Higdon [ASCAP].
Text by Paul Laurence Dunbar.

Measure 25 begins in either B♭ Mixolydian or A♭ Lydian. If this passage is interpreted to be in A♭ Lydian, the salient pitch is a raised fourth scale degree, D♮. This pitch appears on the words "sweet," "Love," and "dear," highlighting the qualities of this kind of love. The music builds intensity on "You are soft as the nesting dove," and then relaxes as the phrase ends, "Come to my heart and bring it to rest, As the bird flies home to its welcome nest." This passage contains rapid arched contours rising and falling in variations, as if in large sighs, expanding and contracting. Any effort to remain grounded within a key is deprioritized in favor of counterpoint and color created through tone clusters. At different times, the different vocal sections assume the lead. For example, the basses rise dramatically in measures 25–26. A decrescendo is made from *f* to *mp* in measure 27 for the words "You are soft," as the sopranos take the lead; they ascend delicately on the text "nesting dove," painting the dove gently lofting overhead. Taking the lead again in measures 29 and 30 (Figure 6-4), the basses ascend on the invitation for love to "Come to my heart," and then descend on "and bring it to rest." In a lovely moment portraying the dove, the tenors, landing on a suspension in measure 33, delay the bird's settling into the nest, and when it settles, they resolve to the final chord. Though the tenor suspension has resolved, the altos create an unresolved B♭^{7} chord, consistent with a B♭ Mixolydian pandiatonic approach.

Figure 6-4. Jennifer Higdon, *Invitation to Love*, mm. 29–33
Music Copyright © 2016 by Jennifer Higdon [ASCAP].
Text by Paul Laurence Dunbar.

The next phrase begins in measure 34 in another new harmonic center: E♭ major. While E♭ major might fit within the context of B♭ Mixolydian from the preceding phrase, it sounds here as a new tonal area and continues through the next main cadence in measure 44, as seen in Figure 6-5. It is important to note that, while Higdon uses different tonal centers to start sections of a poem, these tonal centers often relate to one another. E♭ major is diatonic to and a fourth above B♭ Mixolydian, for example. A previous change of tonal center had occurred in measures 18–19, from a G major triad functioning within the key of C major, moving to F Lydian—again by a diatonic shift of a fourth. In measures 24–25, F Lydian changes to B♭ Mixolydian—another shift of a fourth, though this one is non-diatonic and the tonal centers are in greater contrast with one another. Later, at measure 45, the harmony will again shift up a fourth, from E♭ major to an A♭ major chord, following a cadence on B♭^{6}. A similar harmonic idea will occur in measures 50–51; measure 50 cadences on a B♭^{9} chord, and measure 51 starts on an F minor suspended chord. This is a shift a fifth higher. Surprising harmonic changes like these characterize the work.

Each new section of text unfolds in longer, arched phrases. In measure 34, the melody moves upward on the words "Come when my heart is full of grief," with bitter harmonic seconds on "full of grief." The melody surges up again on "Or when my heart is merry." A climactic moment of text painting occurs at the phrase "Come with the falling, falling of the leaf." The leaf's falling is portrayed in parallel descending thirds in the six upper voices in SAT divisi. The voices move in contrary motion on beat two of measure 42 for a rich cadence on a B♭^{9} chord. On the next line describing the opening of the cherry blossoms, "Or with the redd'ning cherry," the musical phrase itself opens; it begins on a C minor triad and moves through a rising line with stacked seconds to a B♭$^{7/6}$ chord. This kind of moment, in which harmonic densities occur in direct connection with specific text choices, occurs so often in Higdon's music that it is clearly by intention.

Figure 6-5. Jennifer Higdon, *Invitation to Love*, mm. 34–35 and 40–44
Music Copyright © 2016 by Jennifer Higdon [ASCAP].
Text by Paul Laurence Dunbar.

In measure 45 the new tonality centers on an A♭ major triad (Figure 6-6a). This is a somewhat radical move from the previous B♭$^{7/6}$ chord, but though A♭ is the new root, the B♭ Mixolydian mode remains, keeping continuity with the poetry. The male voices begin with a rising, arched form on "Come when the year's first blossom blows." The female voices respond in descending counterpoint with each other a measure later. They depict how the wind blows through the blossoms, through waving motions between lower and higher pitches. The technique is much like that found in measures 19–20.

Figure 6-6a. Jennifer Higdon, *Invitation to Love*, mm. 45–47
Music Copyright © 2016 by Jennifer Higdon [ASCAP].
Text by Paul Laurence Dunbar.

This same structure is repeated in the next phrase, "Come when the summer gleams and glows," which is sung by the male voices with the female voices entering one measure later (Figure 6-6b). This time, the male voices arch downward and female voices, starting lower, rise, weaving through and around the modal tonality to paint the summer's glow.

Figure 6-6b. Jennifer Higdon, *Invitation to Love*, mm. 48–50
Music Copyright © 2016 by Jennifer Higdon [ASCAP].
Text by Paul Laurence Dunbar.

The next entrance on "Come with the winter's drifting snow" is set in SAT divisi and recalls the descending motive for the falling leaf (Figure 6-6c). The male voices now assume the role of commenting, which the female voices held earlier. The bass line descends in imitative counterpoint two beats after the other voices, portraying snowfall.

These three segments in measures 45–53 represent spring, summer, and winter, with three-measure phrases for each one. Higdon varies the texture by alternating entrances of upper versus lower voices, setting one group in homophony while the other responds in counterpoint. The voices remain within the Bb Mixolydian scale.

Figure 6-6c. Jennifer Higdon, *Invitation to Love*, mm. 51–53
Music Copyright © 2016 by Jennifer Higdon [ASCAP].
Text by Paul Laurence Dunbar.

Measure 56 begins the final section of the composition. The text, "You are sweet, O Love, dear Love, You are soft as the nesting dove," is repeated, as is the musical sequence for this earlier phrase from measures 26–33. Set now a minor third higher, the upper voices are in six-part divisi. A new harmonic base, Ab minor, will be retained almost to the end of the work. The basses start in consort with the other voices, then emerge in counterpoint, enhancing the otherwise homophonic texture, consistent with the earlier setting. Chord extensions and added tones contribute to the work's overall lush quality.

With "Come to my heart and bring it to rest As the bird flies home," the basses sing again in arched contours (Figure 6-7). They ascend on "Come to my heart" and descend threading through the other voices on "bring it to rest"; then they rise in an upward sweep portraying the bird's flight. All voices join for "to its welcome nest," the sopranos in an arched phrase, while the others delicately descend to the final cadence. Again, a retardation delays the final chord, as the bird slowly settles into its nest. The cadence occurs on a warm Db major triad; the altos resolve the dominant seventh upward to the root.

Figure 6-7. Jennifer Higdon, *Invitation to Love*, mm. 60–65
Music Copyright © 2016 by Jennifer Higdon [ASCAP].
Text by Paul Laurence Dunbar.

The piece concludes with the final phrase of the poem, which highlights the work's title, "Hear this Invitation to Love" (Figure 6-8). It occurs in Gb major, a tritone away from the work's beginning in C major. These tonal centers are as far away from each other as possible—does this represent the mystery and awe of genuine, deep love?

The final three measures are stunning. The choir moves in gentle parallel motion in a slightly arched contour. The individual syllables of the final stepwise ascent are set in pointillistic counterpoint: syllables are handed off, one voice part to another, forming the complete phrase. In an astonishing piece of text painting, Higdon's setting makes it apparent that the act of accepting this invitation to love must be relational—shared, given, and received.

Figure 6-8. Jennifer Higdon, *Invitation to Love*, mm. 66–70
Music Copyright © 2016 by Jennifer Higdon [ASCAP].
Text by Paul Laurence Dunbar.

Several features of *Invitation to Love* distinguish this work. The phrase lengths are overall longer and more linear than in Higdon's other choral works. Arching contours move upward over several measures, followed by downward trajectories again over several measures. These phrases occur in sequential groups, two or three in a row. In the last section, a substantial amount of text is delivered within ten measures (measures 56–65), all in sequential, arching phrases that rise, fall, and then surge up again. These intensify to a dramatic peak in the last four measures.

The work is dense with added tones and pandiatonicism. A harmonic lushness and warmth envelopes the listener. While a number of micro-harmonic shifts align with specific moments of poetry, there are overarching, macro-harmonies that govern the overall structure. This larger harmonic structure aligns with the poetic form. As the work opens, the pitches of C major prevail until measure 25. The text for this section mentions the sun, moon, stars, and twilight, elements of nature and light as metaphors for a timeless, universal characteristic of love.

The next section differs in both harmony and poetic content. From measure 25, the pitches of B♭ Mixolydian prevail until measure 56. The text changes from the metaphors mentioned above to a characterization of love as a dove. At measure 34, the tonal center shifts to E♭ major, which contains the same pitches as B♭ Mixolydian. This change is aligned with the next piece of poetry, an invitation extended by someone pleading for relief from grief and the passing of time. The speaker refers to the seasons as metaphors for life; the heartfelt sentiments are filled with both nostalgia and gratitude. Within this passage, measure 44 cadences on a B♭$^{7/6}$ chord. An A♭ major triad appears in the male voices at the mention of spring, "Come when the year's first blossom blows." An F minor triad is used in measure 48 for summer, "Come when the summer gleams and glows." F minor is again heard for "Come with the winter's drifting snow," which then cadences on a rich B♭^{11} chord. All of this section remains within the pitches of B♭ Mixolydian.

The peak of the piece occurs as the harmony moves to A♭ minor, which is used in measures 56–65. The text repeats the passage that characterizes love as a nesting dove, but now in a more emphatic musical setting. This section's cadence occurs on the warm triad of D♭ major, the subdominant in an A♭ minor scale.

The final four measures, a coda, begin in C♭ major and end on a G♭ major triad, which are once again both surprising harmonic changes. The text is the final invitation, "Hear this invitation to Love." This harmonic structure creates four overarching musical atmospheres that contextualize the four primary sections of poetry.

Invitation to Love is a piece to drink in deeply; one must breathe with the singers, with the poet. It is a yogic composition—meditative, calming, yet at times exhilarating. At the work's premier, a number of audience members exhaled or sighed, then applauded with deep appreciation when the work finished. That effect rings true to the nature of the poetry.

CHAPTER SEVEN

OUR BEAUTIFUL COUNTRY

Our Beautiful Country, from the opera *Cold Mountain*
(2012/2015) 5 minutes
TTBB a cappella
Text by Gene Scheer (used with his kind permission), secular

Buried and forgotten, in the fields… under trees…
In valleys, and on mountains,
we sing their elegies.
What will echo from our song?
What has changed from this land of toil and pain?
What will grow from this scarlet soil?

We are soldiers, sons, civilians,
we flow, the unnamed tributaries of our nation's blood,
the rivers of our nation's blood.
Buried and forgotten, in our beautiful, beautiful country… where we lie
buried,
We rest beneath every step you take, in the dust,
in the ground on which you tread…
oh, beautiful country.

Hear the echo of our song,
and feel the shadow from our pain and toil,
across the valleys spread in scarlet soil,
our elegies echo loudly…

Hear the brittle snap of twigs, encased in Winter's blackest bark.
The plumb line of our soul's been cracked,
as one by one the stars go dark, in our beautiful country…
in our beautiful country we're buried and forgotten in the fields,
under trees… and on the plains… and in valleys, and on the mountains,
we sing their elegies.
Oh beautiful country, our beautiful country.

Higdon's opera *Cold Mountain* was co-commissioned by the Santa Fe Opera, Opera Philadelphia, and Minnesota Opera in collaboration with the North Carolina Opera. It was completed in 2012. The libretto by Gene Scheer is based on Charles Frazier's novel that takes place in eastern Tennessee and North Carolina during the American Civil War. "Our Beautiful Country" is a male chorus from Act 2, Scene 10 of the opera. The stage directions indicate that soldiers who have perished in the war slowly appear; the expression marking is *Majestic.* Their chorus serves as a moment of deep reflection and remembrance, as the voices from beyond the grave relay their perspectives. Soldiers from both the North and South sing together, conveying the lesson that there are no sides any longer, no more battles to be fought.

When *Cold Mountain* first opened in Santa Fe, Higdon was already considering extracting this chorus for use outside of the opera. She pondered whether the title should come from the chorus's first line, "Buried and forgotten," or its last, "our beautiful country." The latter represented the prevailing essence of the work, in her deduction, and became the title. (These are thoughts she shared with me in person at the work's opening.) The chorus received such recognition and acclaim that Higdon was urged to set it as a stand-alone work, which she did in 2015. While the opera version is accompanied by orchestra and performed by operatic singers, the stand-alone work is more intimate: it is written for a cappella voices and does not contain commentary from the soprano soloist. Higdon also wrote a conclusive ending for the arrangement, whereas the operatic version transitions into an aria.

Our Beautiful Country is composed of clear sections with a recurring refrain: $A^1B^1A^2B^2CA^3$. The musical setting is tonal, consonant, rich, and warm. Throughout most of the piece, the top three voices (TTB) move in homophony while the low basses follow in subtle counterpoint. The basses are a persistent representation of the depth of the grave, the ever-present permanence of death.

The opening words, "Buried and forgotten, in the fields… under trees," are sung by the three upper voices, while the low basses join one beat later (Figure 7-1). The melody winds around the tone of C, the third in the A♭ major tonality, granting some serenity to this mournful opening text.

Figure 7-1. Jennifer Higdon, *Our Beautiful Country*, mm. 1–4
Music Copyright © 2012/2015 by Jennifer Higdon [ASCAP].
Text by Gene Scheer (used with permission).

The soldiers continue, "In valleys, and on the mountains, we sing their elegies" (Figure 7-2). The phrase moves counterintuitively upward for "valleys" and downward for "mountains," but the low basses, in response to the other voices, articulate the "valleys" in a downward line. These first nine measures set a tone of peaceful resignation. The singers represent voices of prophecy for the soldiers still fighting battles.

Figure 7-2. Jennifer Higdon, *Our Beautiful Country*, mm. 5–9
Music Copyright © 2012/2015 by Jennifer Higdon [ASCAP].
Text by Gene Scheer (used with permission).

Next the men raise the question, "What will echo from our song? What has changed from this land of toil and pain?" (Figure 7-3). While the other voices hold the word "echo," the basses create a text-painting effect and repeat the words just sung. The upper voices then rise in angst, acknowledging their own senseless sacrifice. The basses echo the last words, "land of toil and pain."

In the conclusion of the opening, the men continue to vent their desperation: "What will grow from this scarlet soil?" They emphasize "scarlet" in a sharp sixteenth and dotted-eighth rhythm to indicate the violence of bloodshed. The basses, singing in a low range as if buried beneath the soil, rise only slightly when posing the question of "What might grow?" Of what benefit was their personal sacrifice on both sides of this war? What were their deaths worth?

Figure 7-3. Jennifer Higdon, *Our Beautiful Country*, mm. 10–17
Music Copyright © 2012/2015 by Jennifer Higdon [ASCAP].
Text by Gene Scheer (used with permission).

In section B¹, which begins in measure 18, the soldiers seem to come alive as they plead in the present tense, "We are soldiers, sons, civilians, we flow, the unnamed tributaries of our nation's blood, the rivers of our nation's blood" (Figure 7-4). The tonality has shifted to B major, an augmented second, or enharmonic minor third, away from the A♭ major of the first section. The dynamic is a simple *mf*, but in the work's operatic premiere, the chorus sang a crescendo through this passage and began in a tempo that was faster than what came before. The counterpoint is flipped to the high tenors, who now respond to the other singers. The contrapuntal changes may be considered to represent different sides in the war: blue versus gray. Both voices are still unified in a choral offering, as the soldiers were unified as citizens.

The first two notes in the entrance of the second tenor line rise by a perfect fourth—the first interval sounded in taps. The voices surge forward in primarily parallel and homorhythmic motion. The rhythms match natural speech inflections, as for example in the syllabic settings for "civilians," "tributaries," and "nation's." In measure 19, the word "blood" is emphasized through elongation.

After being stated in measure 21, the words "of our nation's blood" are repeated in measures 22–23 with new pitches that create a harmonic vagueness, graphically illustrating the sense of loss. Seconds appear both melodically and harmonically. The melody cascades downward on "rivers of our nation's blood," as the blood soaks into the ground and as the men, once again, settle into their graves. It is of note that, after the B major tonality, Higdon selects E♭ major as the triad of resolution in measure 24. This is quite a departure from traditional harmonic expectations, yet both keys share an enharmonic common tone, D♯/E♭. There is, therefore, a consonant, relative connection between these tonal centers: the two sides of the soldiers are connected to one country as well.

Figure 7-4. Jennifer Higdon, *Our Beautiful Country*, mm. 18–24
Music Copyright © 2012/2015 by Jennifer Higdon [ASCAP].
Text by Gene Scheer (used with permission).

The E♭ cadence prepares the return of the opening music in A♭ major. The A² section begins with the same music on the words "Buried and forgotten in our beautiful country," but alterations soon emerge. The tenors echo "where we lie buried" in a descant-like fashion in parallel thirds. As shown in Figure 7-5, all four parts merge into chant-like and lofting tessituras, offering a ghostly message to the living: "We rest beneath every step you take, in the dust, in the ground on which you tread…" For the last part of that phrase, all the voices move downward as if toward the ground.

Figure 7-5. Jennifer Higdon, *Our Beautiful Country*, mm. 28–32
Music Copyright © 2012/2015 by Jennifer Higdon [ASCAP].
Text by Gene Scheer (used with permission).

In the B^2 section, the text is "Hear the echo of our song, and feel the shadow from our pain and toil, across the valley spread in scarlet soil, our elegies echo loudly" (Figure 7-6). By being set in B major like the first B section and using similar rhythms, the music echoes the text. The return of B major when the soldiers sing "Here the echo of our song" is something of a harmonic leitmotiv. This is one of the most impassioned portions of the score. The choir's vocal range expands in both directions: the tenors soar higher and the basses dig deeper. The rhythms become shorter, more complex, and more contrapuntal. The basses, as usual, have the most active line of counterpoint.

In text and mood painting, echoes are echoed, and the sense of shadow is portrayed through a deepening of the bass line. The piece's first passages of shorter rhythms of consecutive sixteenth notes convey the anxiety of the soldiers over their senseless loss of life. Changing meters, alternating between 3/4 and 2/4 for eight measures, exploit instability to depict pain and toil. The words "pain" and "toil" are emphasized with the relatively sustained rhythm of dotted-eighth notes in measure 36.

There is desperation in the voices of these dead men. Along with despair and angst, frustration is felt at their sacrifice. They now realize, in death, that they are unified, regardless of which cause they fought for. It no longer matters if they wore blue or gray, or for what flag they died.

Figure 7-6. Jennifer Higdon, *Our Beautiful Country*, mm. 33–36
Music Copyright © 2012/2015 by Jennifer Higdon [ASCAP].
Text by Gene Scheer (used with permission).

The next text, "Across the valleys spread in scarlet soil, our elegies echo loudly," is elided with the previous phrase and moves into A Lydian, which shares six out of seven pitches with the B major scale which came before. The text refers to "our elegies," as the dead men speak in a collective first person. Elsewhere, near the beginning and end of the piece, the text is rather "their elegies," indicating homage to all the men lost in the war.

The next phrase contains new music, a C section or bridge that ends the A^1, B^1, A^2, B^2 binary form found thus far. The harmony in measure 40 shifts down a half step to A♭ Lydian with chromatic influences. The soldiers, singing from their graves, respond to the living walking above them: "Hear the brittle snap of twigs, encased in Winter's blackest bark." This moment is intensely personal and heartbreaking. According to history, there was little or no fighting during the winter in the American Civil War, meaning that these men would have died months earlier.

These are broken men; in desperation they sing, "The plumb line of our soul's been cracked, as one by one, the stars go dark, in our beautiful country" (Figure 7-7). This section is a peak of the work; the tenors sing in their highest tessitura in the piece. The full chorus is set in close, tight chromatic harmonies and added-tone chords with seconds; the sounds condense and unify in this powerful section. The independent bass lines are not present here; the texture is primarily homorhythmic. Text painting is ever-present. Notably, the melody rises steeply on "our soul's been cracked" as the harmony moves to an unresolved B♭^{7} chord; this represents a metaphorical cracking of their souls. On the text "as one by one the stars go dark," the voices leap downward to convey this loss. The harmony here returns to an A♭ grounding for the final refrain.

Figure 7-7. Jennifer Higdon, *Our Beautiful Country*, mm. 43–47
Music Copyright © 2012/2015 by Jennifer Higdon [ASCAP].
Text by Gene Scheer (used with permission).

The third and final refrain, or A section, is almost identical to the opening measures; the men sing, "in our beautiful country we're buried and forgotten in the fields, under trees…" This time, there is more commenting and response among the voices. The bass line resumes its contrapuntal response role.

Whether in homophony or counterpoint, all the voices have elongated rhythmic values near the end of the piece, as shown in Figure 7-8. The harmonic rhythm is also slowed and almost entirely arrested. In the final three measures, Higdon moves through Db major to Eb major and rests on an Ab major triad on the words "beautiful country" as the soldiers return to their rest.

Figure 7-8. Jennifer Higdon, *Our Beautiful Country*, mm. 58–62
Music Copyright © 2012/2015 by Jennifer Higdon [ASCAP].
Text by Gene Scheer (used with permission).

Our Beautiful Country is set in two alternating tonal centers, Ab major and B major. Ab major can be heard as a warm, rich, darker hue, especially in male voices, while B major is brighter. The B major sections bring the tenors to soaring high notes and take the basses out of their lower region during the more hopeful sections of text.

The piece is largely homophonic; the chords line up as soldiers in a platoon formation, joined rhythmically and harmonically as one unit, and no longer separated into two military units. The bass line counterpoint that emanates from the lower reaches of the chorus is perhaps symbolic of the soldiers in the grave, and certainly, its presence gives a gravity and depth of character to the music.

Do not be misled into thinking that this is an accessible, fairly simple piece. Its inner complexities, intricately woven lines, and demanding tunings underscore the angst of killing and loss. But the ultimate message is one of unity—melodic, harmonic, textural—achieved through poetry. The piece is resolute and a beautiful depiction of mourning from the men who sacrificed their lives for our beautiful country.

CHAPTER EIGHT

O MAGNUM MYSTERIUM

O magnum mysterium
(2002) about 8 minutes
SATB choir scored for 2 crystal glasses, 2 flutes, and chimes
Other settings available: a cappella and with organ accompaniment
Commissioned by the Philadelphia Singers, David Hayes, Music Director
Sacred, Christmas

O magnum mysterium,	*O great mystery*
et admirabile sacramentum,	*and wondrous sacrament,*
ut animalia viderent Dominum natum	*that animals might see the newborn Lord*
jacentem in praesepio.	*lying in a manger.*
Beata Virgo	*Blessed is the Virgin,*
cujus viscera meruerunt	*whose womb was worthy*
portare Dominum Christum.	*to bear the Lord Christ.*

O magnum mysterium is a Latin responsorial chant in use since before the tenth century. The text, which describes Christ's nativity and his being laid in a manger surrounded by animals, appears to be based on passages from Scripture; it has long been a part of the matins service for Christmas in the Catholic tradition.

Higdon has published three arrangements of the text: one for a cappella choir, another in the traditional church instrumentation of SATB choir with organ accompaniment, and a third for SATB choir in divisi with two flutes, two crystal glasses, and chimes. It is this last setting that is the focus in this chapter, as its instrumentation presents a new outlook and distinctive relationship to the text. The arrangement is eclectic. Higdon draws on early music by using open fifths, parallel motion, church modes, and chant-like passages in reference to medieval music and particularly thirteenth-century organum. She surrounds these elements with contemporary instrumentation. Flutes and crystal glasses create atmospheres of a world beyond. The chimes recall church bells and the handbell choirs that can be found in church services. For a more contemporary sound, Higdon infuses the piece with neotonality and added seconds.

The piece is in ternary form, ABA', plus an introduction for choir and crystal glasses and an instrumental bridge before the A' section. The tripartite structure can in the Christian faith be interpreted to represent the Holy Trinity, a symbolism Johann Sebastian Bach used often. The three-part setting of the text spans the ancient and the modern: the A section uses the ancient Latin of the traditional Catholic church, the B section modern English, and the A' section Latin again.

Introduction

Throughout the introduction, the crystal glasses hold the pitches D and A, which establish the key and recall the mystical ringing open fifths of medieval music (Figure 8-1a). The lower three voices of the choir (ATB) enter singing "O" on a D major triad. These ten measures create an atmosphere of the unknown, the unexplainable spiritual offering referred to in the text "O magnum mysterium."

In measure 7, the flutes reinforce the open fifth of D and A with offbeat accents. In measure 9, they move to G and D, expanding into a stack of fifths with the glasses. In measure 10, they move to A and E, creating a new harmony, a consonant $C^{6/9}$ chord.

The words "O magnum mysterium" are sung in a chant-like melody by the sopranos in measure 8 (Figure 8-1b). The choir undulates between C major and D major triads in parallel organum-like motion beneath the glasses' open fifth. Though the harmony imitates early music, it also contains modern polytonal allusions. For example, the sopranos enter on the nonharmonic tone G when the rest of the choir is on a D major triad. The sopranos join the rest of the choir in D major in measure 9, but when the choir undulates back to C major, the sopranos change to D, another discordant color note. All parts resolve to a C^6 as the introduction concludes in measure 10.

Figure 8-1a. Jennifer Higdon, *O magnum mysterium*, mm. 1–5
Music Copyright © 2002 by Jennifer Higdon [ASCAP].

Figure 8-1b. Jennifer Higdon, *O magnum mysterium*, mm. 6–10
Music Copyright © 2002 by Jennifer Higdon [ASCAP].

Section A

The first A section begins in D Mixolydian as the sopranos weave around F♯ in chant-like, mostly stepwise motion (Figure 8-2). The rest of the choir moves in contrary motion against the soprano line. They start on a D major triad, with an open fifth between the tenor and bass; they then move in parallel stepwise motion to C major and then B♭ major, in considerable harmonic contrast to the soprano line. These neotonal harmonies, D–C–B♭ … C–B♭–Am–B♭–C–D, against the D Mixolydian melody, yield an unstable, other-worldly character. The cross-relation of F and F♯ on the downbeat of measure 13 aids in this purpose but also harkens to medieval music, in which such cross-relations could be expected. At the cadence in measures 14–15 the sopranos' C creates a D⁷. The flutes dance above in amorphous, colorful texturing. These elements together produce a contemporary harmonic fabric with early music references.

Figure 8-2. Jennifer Higdon, *O magnum mysterium*, mm. 11–15
Music Copyright © 2002 by Jennifer Higdon [ASCAP].

The choir is in homophony for "ut animalia viderent Dominum Natum, jacentem in praesepio" (Figure 8-3). The sopranos move in an arched contour in measures 16–20 and again in measures 21–15, reflecting the earlier chant-like line from measures 11–14. The lower three voices move in stepwise, parallel triads that imitate parallel organum. These voices contrast with the soprano line by mirroring its contour throughout this section.

Figure 8-3. Jennifer Higdon, *O magnum mysterium*, pickup to mm. 16–20
Music Copyright © 2002 by Jennifer Higdon [ASCAP].

The end of the above phrase, "jacentem in praesepio," which in English means "lying in a manger," is repeated and sequenced in fragments to build to a peak. In the final iteration, the rhythms become larger and the meter changes from 2/4 to 3/4 and 4/4 to elongate the phrase (Figure 8-4). This becomes *Augenmusik*, or eye-music: the score shows the vocal lines lying down, descending and reposing, as the child is lying in the manger. The flutes also descend with the voices in measures 27–28. Like the preceding phrase, this section cadences on a D⁷. The remaining open fifth on D and A in the flutes and crystal glasses, which they have held since the beginning, recalls the opening.

Figure 8-4. Jennifer Higdon, *O magnum mysterium*, pickup to mm. 25–32
Music Copyright © 2002 by Jennifer Higdon [ASCAP].

Section B and Instrumental Bridge

The English section of the work begins with a surprising harmonic shift from D major to B♭ major in measure 33 (Figure 8-5). In the first phrase of text, "O great mystery and wondrous sacrament," B♭s and G major triads occur on the words "wondrous sacrament" and create a striking tonal hue in the otherwise B♭ tonal region. This section is a cappella and homochoral. The dynamic begins in *p* and is shaped with hairpins that coincide with the harmonic motion and phrase structure. The chant-like arched contours persist, but the voices now move in parallel motion, in contrast to earlier when the sopranos moved in contrary motion to the organum-like passages in the lower voices (see Figure 8-3, for example).

Figure 8-5. Jennifer Higdon, *O magnum mysterium,* pickup to mm. 33–36
Music Copyright © 2002 by Jennifer Higdon [ASCAP].

The phrase "newborn Lord lying in a manger" is sung five times, building in imitative fashion to convey a growing sense of awe at this sight. The first two phrases begin in B♭, shifting to G major on "newborn Lord," becoming more emphatic on each repeat. The rhythmic values become shorter when sixteenth notes appear in all voices in homorhythm (Figure 8-6). In measure 45, the rhythms elongate, a crescendo is introduced, and the male voices ascend to the peak in measure 46 where the seven-part divisi choir bursts out in an abundance of harmonic seconds on the text "Blessed is the Virgin." The flutes return with their flourishes, and the chimes ring, as indicated in the score, *randomly in any rhythm and order (as if church bells)*. It is a High Church moment and a climax of the piece. Higdon portrays a glorious celebration honoring the Virgin Mary and exulting in the miraculous birth, the arrival of God in human form.

Figure 8-6. Jennifer Higdon, *O magnum mysterium*, mm. 44–48
Music Copyright © 2002 by Jennifer Higdon [ASCAP].

The tonal center continues in B♭ colored with major sevenths. The upper voices repeat "Jesus Christ, the Lord," while the basses punctuate the word "Lord" on the fourth beats in measures 49 and 50, underscoring that this newborn baby is indeed Lord (Figure 8-7a). The chords change again from B♭ to G major and then to an unprepared A♭ triad, a surprising harmonic color, in measure 52 in the text's third iteration.

Figure 8-7a. Jennifer Higdon, *O magnum mysterium*, mm. 49–52
Music Copyright © 2002 by Jennifer Higdon [ASCAP].

The chimes are instructed to slow their rhythm in measure 50, and they resolve to a single repeated tone in measure 53, continuing to imitate a church bell. The voices arrive on a G major final cadence for this middle section. The musical setting brings reverence, reflection, and a sense of soulful assurance to the text.

In the instrumental bridge, the flutes reenter on open fifths, G and D, consonant with the choir, but as the choir holds their chord, the flutes move to other sets of fifths, first Eb–Bb and then C–G. The effect contributes to the aesthetic of the truly unknown, an inexplicable spiritual affirmation. Providing a moment of meditative reflection, the chimes and flutes return to the ideas that began the piece.

Figure 8-7b. Jennifer Higdon, *O magnum mysterium*, mm. 50–54
Music Copyright © 2002 by Jennifer Higdon [ASCAP].

A′ Section

A new Latin text brings in the third and final section in measure 59: "O magnum mysterium Beata Virgo cujus viscera meruerunt portare Dominum Christum" (Blessed is the Virgin, whose womb was worthy to bear the Lord Christ). Like in the chant-like opening, the male voices enter on G and C and move in parallel motion, descending by a whole step and then returning to the starting pitch (Figure 8-8a); it is a similar undulation as heard earlier but now in fifths instead of triads. The altos enter a few measures later and move in parallel motion with the male voices. The crystal glasses reenter at the same time and recall the original tonal center of D major. Finally, the sopranos join, also harkening back to the opening.

Figure 8-8a. Jennifer Higdon, *O magnum mysterium*, mm. 59–64
Music Copyright © 2002 by Jennifer Higdon [ASCAP].

In measure 64, the music departs from the parallel fifths and chant references. F♯s appear in conjunction with C major triads, juxtaposed with F♮s in a back and forth conversation of aural instability. The furthest outlying harmony in the piece is the deep A♭ chord in measure 67, which arrives as the basses reach their lowest notes in the phrase. The chord is placed on the word "viscera," or womb (Figure 8-8b). This harmonic depth metaphorically resembles the depth of the womb. In an impactful moment of word painting, the entire choir descends to the word "viscera" and ascends again, indicating the event of the birth.

Figure 8-8b. Jennifer Higdon, *O magnum mysterium*, mm. 63–67
Music Copyright © 2002 by Jennifer Higdon [ASCAP].

The piece's most volatile harmonic section occurs on "Beata Virgo portare Dominum Christum" (Blessed is the Virgin, who bears the Lord Christ). Here the harmony conveys the mystery of the incarnation. The last words of the phrase, "Dominum Christum," are repeated four times while the phrase climbs to a climax through the series of chord changes labeled in Figure 8-9. The harmonic rhythm is fast, and the harmonies themselves are adventurous and unstable. The strong arrival on the final "Dominum Christum" is the second and ultimate peak of the piece. The sopranos soar to a high A while the inner lines move in counterpoint.

Over measures 79–81, the bottom three voices decrescendo and descend in parallel whole steps through the triads D–C–Bb–Ab, then ascend to Bb and C; the lowest two voices move in open fifths. The progression D–C–Bb in measures 79–80 is a characterizing harmonic sequence in this work. The opening chant line returns in measure 82, bringing the F♯ into play in C Lydian, which furthers an ascending aural quality.

Figure 8-9. Jennifer Higdon, *O magnum mysterium*, mm. 72–82
Music Copyright © 2002 by Jennifer Higdon [ASCAP].

This return to the opening line forms a codetta that frames the work. The tenors and basses sing in parallel, organum-like fifths and polytonal allusions; their tonal centers are somewhat independent of the female voices—adding to the mystery in this moment. The altos are coupled with the sopranos in what becomes a duet in counterpoint with the low voices (Figure 8-10). Above the choir, the crystal glasses resume their open fifth of D and A, as the flutes decorate the texture with ethereal, sparsely written ascensions. This section gives the aural impression of C Lydian, but the two upper voices outline D major.

The final measures culminate in an eclectic harmonic mix. From
measure 90, the sopranos and altos move together in thirds and in measure
92 arrive alone on B♭ major. The tenors and basses reenter in measure 93
on D major, and the altos add the minor seventh on the second beat. The
sopranos and altos then pass through a tritone, C–F♯, in the sopranos'
anticipation before the cadence on D major. All voices alternate on various
beats and continue to adjust through the final measure. Above them, the
crystal glasses still ring, and the flutes give the final quiet punctuation on
an ephemeral D–A fifth, as they began. The music leaves the listener with
a sense of wonder, mystery, and quiet majesty.

Figure 8-10. Jennifer Higdon, *O magnum mysterium*, mm. 86–95
Music Copyright © 2002 by Jennifer Higdon [ASCAP].

CHAPTER NINE

ALLELUIA

Alleluia
(2016) 4 minutes
SATB a cappella
For the Mendelssohn Club of Philadelphia, Phil Rardin, Artistic Director
Text by Jennifer Higdon, sacred

Sing We Sing Hear Us Sing
We Sing this Song
And Let us give With this song
And Let us sing With this song
Let us give Let us sing allelu, alleluia,

Let us give thanks for all we sing in song,
Rejoice through song.
Alle..., alle..., ...luia, ...luia.
We give thanks in our song.
We rejoice. Sing... Alleluia
We praise... Let the bells peal their song...
And hear bells ring, that ring Alleluia

Let the bells ring Alleluia...
Let us give thanks through the wonder of the sung word.
Sing we now in praise with voices that ring like a joyous bell!
Oh praise the word that sings of joy,
Alleluia.

We sing alleluia
Let us give thanks through wonder of, joy of song.
Let our voices sing out, Alleluia.
Sing these praises, song, let us hear the bells...
Sing this alleluia, Alleluia,
Let us give thanks for all the light and the song we share...
Alleluia

Hear us sing these words for you,
Alleluia!

Jennifer Higdon's *Alleluia* was written in honor of Alan Harler, a distinguished choral conductor of twenty-seven years with the Mendelssohn Club of Philadelphia. "The Mendelssohn Club commissioned a series of works called the *Alleluias for Alan*," Higdon explains. "All of these works had to incorporate the word 'Alleluia' in some way, and this work was the result."[1] She wrote her *Alleluia* to celebrate the joys of singing and of creating a community through song.

Countless musical settings of the word "Alleluia" or "Hallelujah" have been written throughout history. Higdon's is substantial, much like the settings of Randall Thompson, George Frideric Handel, or Ludwig van Beethoven. But it is also innovative and unlike the others in a number of ways. One aspect that sets it apart is that Higdon crafted additional lyrics, as seen above. Her text is delivered in fragments as the work unfolds in a through-composed form.

In this chapter, the work is analyzed by sections that are not delineated in Higdon's score. An overview follows:

Section 1 (mm. 1–28): an extended, pointillistic introduction
Section 2 (mm. 29–35): a homophonic peak
Section 3 (mm. 36–38): a bridge to the next substantive section
Section 4 (mm. 39–70): an extended development, incorporating ideas put forth thus far
Section 5 (mm. 71–83): another peak, in counterpoint for double chorus
Section 6 (mm. 84–107): a second developmental section, incorporating the opening motives and a new leaping theme
Section 7 (mm. 107–125): an extended coda that builds upon the theme from Section 6, with stretto counterpoint to the end

As is evident in this overview, the composition's evolution is complex. Nonetheless all of the musical ideas are intimately coupled with the text, as detailed below.

Section 1 (mm. 1–28)

Alleluia opens with rhythmic, pointillistic articulations on the syllables of the word "Alleluia" alternating among the vocal parts. The meter is 3/4, a meter often associated with dance, and the key is F Lydian.

The sopranos start on a repeated F and gradually begin to alternate with E. The line expands in a weaving stepwise motion that keeps returning to the home tone of F. The sopranos ultimately aim to sing "Hear

---

[1]   Jennifer Higdon, email to the author, August 12, 2020.

Us Sing, We Sing this Song," but they do so in repeated fragments through measure 27. They simultaneously interpolate this phrase with individual syllables of the word "Alleluia." They begin with "lu" and add other syllables one by one (see Figure 9-1).

The syllables "Lu-La-Lay" are also articulated in the voices that accompany the sopranos. Each syllable is delivered in a bell-like fashion, creating an atmosphere of celebration. The nonsense syllables so far create an impression that the celebration is something that lacks a literal meaning; it is a celebration by, and of, vocal colors and rhythms.

Finally, the sopranos sing the entire word "Alleluia" without interruption in measure 28, the final measure of the introduction. This introduction is longer and more complex than customarily seen in a four-minute a cappella piece. It is a substantial unit of music that sets the piece's tone. The soprano line rises over the last three measures to link to the next section.

Figure 9-1. Jennifer Higdon, *Alleluia*, mm. 6–12
Music Copyright © 2016 by Jennifer Higdon [ASCAP].
Text by Jennifer Higdon.

Section 2 (mm. 29–35)

The voices abandon the broken syllables of "Alleluia" and gather to a glorious peak in seven-part homophony in the key of D major (Figure 9-2). It is both a musical and a communal gathering of voices, aligning with the text "Let us give thanks."

With the introduction of G♯s in measure 30, the mode becomes D
Lydian. The bass and then the alto fill in the homophonic context with
internal running eighth notes that increase the forward motion and density.
Harmonic seconds are formed at the end of the phrase "for all we sing in
song, lay-lu-ia, Rejoice through song." The homophony, modal change,
and seven-part writing all collaborate to convey rejoicing.

Figure 9-2. Jennifer Higdon, *Alleluia*, mm. 29–32
Music Copyright © 2016 by Jennifer Higdon [ASCAP].
Text by Jennifer Higdon.

Section 3 (mm. 36–38)

A short return to the lyric "Alleluia" is set in the women's voices (Figure 9-3). The conversation between the altos and sopranos is offbeat and unpredictable; the sopranos deliver the first two syllables of "Alleluia" and the altos add the last two to form the whole word. Their lines descend, easing into the next section.

Figure 9-3. Jennifer Higdon, *Alleluia*, mm. 36–38
Music Copyright © 2016 by Jennifer Higdon [ASCAP].
Text by Jennifer Higdon.

Section 4 (mm. 39–70)

At the center of the work is the composition's most substantial portion, a thirty-one-measure development. The sopranos and altos continue taking turns to deliver syllables of the word "Alleluia." Accompanied by the women's voices, the tenors begin a new theme on the text "We give thanks in our song. We rejoice. Sing… now… Let the bells peal" (Figure 9-4). The leaps of a fourth in the theme represent the ringing of bells. Stretching from measures 39 to 44, this theme is conceptually, though not literally, a retrograde of the sopranos' ascending line in measures 24–28. The tenors descend, increasing the range of their melody motive by motive through intervallic expansion over an octave, D4 to D3.

Figure 9-4. Jennifer Higdon, *Alleluia*, mm. 39–42
Music Copyright © 2016 by Jennifer Higdon [ASCAP].
Text by Jennifer Higdon.

As the tenors complete their phrase in measure 43, the basses enter on a low B. Their entrance brings harmonic ambiguity against the previous tonal center of E that was present over measures 36–42. The bass line by itself is in C Lydian, but the tenors emphasize B as well. The varying roots and counterpoint make it challenging to analyze the passage in terms of traditional scales. Higdon is known for the neotonality in her instrumental compositions; the same label describes this section of music, which is more harmonically free than most of her other choral writing.

The basses offer a theme that is more linear than the broken lines of the other voices (Figure 9-5). The tenors interpolate elements of both the English lyrics and the Latin *alleluia*.

Figure 9-5. Jennifer Higdon, *Alleluia*, mm. 50–56
Music Copyright © 2016 by Jennifer Higdon [ASCAP].
Text by Jennifer Higdon.

In measure 56, the sopranos sing a lyric theme that recalls the piece's opening, while the basses sing a slower descending melody (Figure 9-6). This begins a contrapuntal, lyric duet in contrary motion between the outer voices. The altos and tenors sing in offbeat relationship to each other, creating a polyrhythmic effect against the basses' grounding quarter notes and contrasting with the lyric soprano line. All the voices repeat "Alleluia" in different iterations of rhythm and melody. The scale is E Aeolian (E–F♯–G–A–B–C–D) in measures 56–57, followed by A melodic minor (A–B–C–D–E–F♯–G♯), though in each case the sequence of tones is free so that no clear root emerges as the basic tonal center. This is a perfect example of the modal mixing common in Higdon's works.

Figure 9-6. Jennifer Higdon, *Alleluia*, mm. 56–60
Music Copyright © 2016 by Jennifer Higdon [ASCAP].
Text by Jennifer Higdon.

As this section evolves, quarter notes give way to eighth notes, and repeated offbeat entrances occur in imitation between the alto and tenor voices. The soprano develops into an independent line with shifting offbeat rhythms. Pandiatonicism continues to be used. The counterpoint incorporates stacked harmonic seconds, and an immense heightening of tension leads to a climax in measure 71 (Figure 9-7).

Figure 9-7. Jennifer Higdon, *Alleluia*, mm. 66–71
Music Copyright © 2016 by Jennifer Higdon [ASCAP].
Text by Jennifer Higdon.

Section 5 (mm. 71–83)

The passage at measure 71 is monumental in the context of the piece. Using the previous section as a springboard, the chorus augments to a double chorus: the female voices function as one homophonic chorus and the male voices as the other. The two engage in a contrapuntal duet on the words "Let us give thanks through the wonder of the sung word." The men offer portions of text that are similar to what the women sing but are musically independent. In the next line, "Sing we now in praise with voices that ring like a joyous bell!" the women present the text unbroken, while the men sing fragments: "We now sing, we bring praise" (Figure 9-8). They join on "that ring like joyous…" The varying assignments of texts and rhythms combine with neotonality to build to a high point.

In measure 80, the voices collect on the words "Oh praise" and relax into a diminuendo for "the word that sings of joy." It is a perfect moment to highlight, since this work is about the joy of singing together.

Figure 9-8. Jennifer Higdon, *Alleluia*, mm. 75–83
Music Copyright © 2016 by Jennifer Higdon [ASCAP].
Text by Jennifer Higdon.

Section 6 (mm. 84–107)

The textures thin out and recall the opening. This framing of the song might lead listeners to deduce that the piece is ending. Instead, this section bridges to the final significant portion of the work. It is merely the calm before the final storm.

At the beginning of the bridge, the altos, in a divisi ostinato, sing quiet

dotted-quarter-note alterations between adjacent pitches; each line starts
on different pitches and at different beats in the measure (Figure 9-9). The
key is D Dorian at first, but in Higdonesque fashion, pitches outside that
mode soon appear.

   A contrasting motive is introduced in measure 86. It is lyrical, arching,
and built on leaps of fifths and fourths. It begins in the soprano but is
echoed in stretto by the basses one measure later. The tenors imitate the
theme two measures later. The text is "We sing Alleluia." "Alleluia" is
now sung in every voice without interruptions or pointillistic alternations.

   These measures incorporate extensive imitative polyphony and shifting
rhythmic accentuations. Some voices are aligned with the written 3/4
meter, but the ostinatos in the altos, for example, are written on offbeats.
Each of the divisi alto lines sounds in 6/8 meter, with two strong beats per
measure; the lower line is offset one eighth note later than the upper. This
creates a polyrhythmic effect once again. A homophonic, chordal cadence
occurs in measure 97.

Figure 9-9. Jennifer Higdon, *Alleluia*, mm. 84–92
Music Copyright © 2016 by Jennifer Higdon [ASCAP].
Text by Jennifer Higdon.

This section began rooted on D and has since moved through other harmonies to arrive on a G♭ major triad, an enharmonic major third above D, in measure 97. This aligns with the text, "Let us give thanks through the wonder of song." G♭ major persists as a tonal center, with an abundance of added tones, for several measures. In measure 101, "Let our voices sing out," the tonal center again changes, from G♭ major to a brief A major triad, another root movement of an enharmonic third (Figure 9-10). This shifts to a polychordal allusion in measure 102 on an E major triad over an open-fifth D chord in the divisi bass lines. A cadence on that same polychord occurs in measure 103. The harmonic rhythm is not yet ready to slow. It moves to C major in measure 104. Measure 105 starts on a C dominant seventh chord and moves to D♭ major for a measure; the lines ascend in parallel to F Mixolydian in measure 107. This measure, with its text "let us hear the bells," lands on a sharp *fp* to imitate the sound when a bell is struck. The downbeat of measure 107 brings the conclusion of Section 6 elided with the opening of Section 7.

Figure 9-10. Jennifer Higdon, *Alleluia*, mm. 101–107
Music Copyright © 2016 by Jennifer Higdon [ASCAP].
Text by Jennifer Higdon.

Section 7 (mm. 107–125)

This is the beginning of the end, in what might be considered an extended coda distinguished by the prominent use of stretto. The voices imitate each other in rising pyramidic fashion, B–T–A–S, four times over measures 107, 110, 116, and 119, the last one expanding in augmentation. Stretto occurs again in measure 123 in reverse, moving from the high voices to low. The celebration is in full throttle as the euphoric *alleluias* pile on top of one another in layered and active counterpoint.

On the first occurrence of stretto, the voices sing, "Sing this alleluia," in F Mixolydian. Higdon takes inspiration from the lyric theme in measures 85–86. The melody contains leaps of fourths and fifths but is set in 4/4 meter instead of the earlier 3/4 meter (Figure 9-11). The melody is not couched in a calm arching legato as before, but is rhythmic, accented in *mf*, and builds entrance by entrance.

Figure 9-11. Jennifer Higdon, *Alleluia*, mm. 107–109
Music Copyright © 2016 by Jennifer Higdon [ASCAP].
Text by Jennifer Higdon.

In measure 112, choral homophony occurs on an E♭ major triad, which is built on the seventh scale degree of F Mixolydian. At the same time, D♭s are introduced, creating modal ambiguity (Figure 9-12). The six upper voices sing, "Let us give thanks for all the light and the song we sing." The bass line incorporates running eighth notes in measures 112–113, decorating the word "thanks." Measure 116 is the fourth and final iteration of the melody that uses leaps of fourths and fifths.

Figure 9-12. Jennifer Higdon, *Alleluia*, mm. 112–116
Music Copyright © 2016 by Jennifer Higdon [ASCAP].
Text by Jennifer Higdon.

Approaching the end, the voices increase in dynamic levels and activity. In measure 121, they come together on the rich harmonic color of a D♭ major triad, a tonal center based on the flatted sixth of F. See Figure 9-13.

The final three measures begin grounded on F—the starting pitch of this work. The voices move through a final pyramidic counterpoint that occurs in reverse, starting in the high voices and cascading downward. All voices arrive on a Db major triad in measure 124, then ascend in parallel motion to an Eb major triad, concluding on an F major triad. This final chord is the ultimate peak of the work. The culminating exuberant reiterations of "Alleluia" provide an exhilarating finish. The piece is vigorous, enthusiastic, spirited, and a true salute to music and the joy of singing.

Figure 9-13. Jennifer Higdon, *Alleluia*, mm. 121–125
Music Copyright © 2016 by Jennifer Higdon [ASCAP].
Text by Jennifer Higdon.

CHAPTER TEN

TELEGRAM

Telegram
(2014) 6 minutes
SATB a cappella
For the Yale Glee Club
Poetry by Jeanne Minahan (2012), secular

Telegram to my Career
Not what I meant or thought.
Weather fine. Come home soon.

Telegram from my Career
Splendors untold.
Rain. Will write again.

Telegram from the Past
You left a paintbrush, wet.
Send cash.

Telegram from the Future
Now you have money.
Bring paintbrush & more time.

Telegram from the Canary
It's not bad so far.

Telegram from Sancho Panza
I'm starting to see things.
Pack more wine.

Telegram from my feet
Lighten up!

Telegram from the Sky
I'm the limit.

Telegram from Last Week
I can never catch up.

Telegram from Next Week
They won't let me wait.

Telegram Smelling Suspiciously of Rum and Coconut
from the Hour lost at the end of Daylight Savings Time
This time I'm not coming back.

Telegram from the Book
left under the Covers
Do you read me?

Telegram from Cleopatra
Marc's fine.
Boat race tomorrow.

Telegram to Last Week
I'll carry you with me.

Telegram to Next Week
Wait.

Telegram from Elvis
Nice shoes.

Telegram to your Lips
Kiss me.

Telegram to the Hour from Daylight Savings Time
(Smelling Suspiciously of Rum and Coconut)
Flight booked. Joining you next week.

Telegram from the Telegram Office
Buy yourself a cell phone.

Telegram from the Library
Silence, please.

Telegram to the President
Peace, peace, peace.

Telegram to Emily Dickinson
We quote you now: Roses, Bees, but—
Yours the Nectar—yours the Dash—

Telegram to God
Message received.

Telegram from Summer
Have you forgotten me?

Telegram from Fall
I've changed.

Telegram from Winter
Be there, soon.

Telegram from Hope
Spring's eternal.

In creating her choral music, Jennifer Higdon is inspired by various genres of poetry, and it is not atypical that she would choose a poem that incorporates an abundance of short and varied sections of text, such as Jeanne Minahan's poem *Telegram: A Recently Discovered Correspondence*. This poem is formed of twenty-six one- or two-line telegrams from, or to, various fanciful sources—for example, "My Career," "Next Week," and "Cleopatra." The poetry is delivered as if someone has gone to a trunk filled with old telegrams and pulled out some at random to read aloud. The composite format of the poem lends itself to varied musical ideas and opportunities for music-text relationships that can change every few measures. *Telegram* may in fact be the ideal piece in which to explore music–text relationship from Higdon's repertoire of small-form, and especially a cappella, works.

The first piece assessed in this book, *The Singing Rooms*, also contained texts by Minahan. It thus seems fitting to frame the book with another Higdon and Minahan collaboration. This analysis of *Telegram* also ends this book because the piece incorporates many elements of Higdon's approach to the music-text relationship and can exemplify her choral works.

The structure of *Telegram* is through-composed to follow the string of messages that are sent to and from various figurative entities, avatars, and illusions. Higdon crafts each in short musical segments. Each is given a distinct character determined by the type of message. Throughout the piece, a pervasive rhythmic ostinato represents the tapping of a teletype machine. This ostinato is expressed as "dot, dot, dot," and occasionally "digga dot," in one or more of the voices. Normally the teletype ostinato enters as soon as each telegram is delivered, so as to link it with the next. As each telegram becomes a piece in a musical patchwork quilt, the ostinati of the teletype machine are the stitches that hold it all together.

The relatively short and always changing motives, tonal centers, and typing sounds work together to create a strong sense of anticipation in this piece. Higdon is not about to let the listener's attention be diverted. Each telegram is cryptic yet evokes an entire story with just a few words.

The first telegram is sent to "my Career." The choir moves in homochoral fashion; then in measures 2 and 4, the tenors initiate the teletype machine motive (Figure 10-1). The key is C major until it becomes C Lydian with the entrance of F♯ in measure 3. The F♯s appear in tight, secundal harmony alternations between the sopranos and altos. Higdon sets this dissonance on text that identifies the bitterly dashed hopes of a career that is "not what I meant or thought." The tapping ostinato reenters, and the work is off and running as the first telegram has been sent.

Figure 10-1. Jennifer Higdon, *Telegram*, mm. 1–4
Music Copyright © 2014 by Jennifer Higdon [ASCAP].
Poem by Jeanne Minahan (2012).

The next telegram is a reply from "my Career": "Splendors untold. Rain. Will write again" (Figure 10-2). The sopranos ascend in a nearly octatonic scale (the last note is a half step higher than expected) on the words "Splendors untold," as if conveying the career's anxious hope that it might be climbing to better things. But the reality is less thrilling. Rain has somehow interrupted the writing of this telegram; the tonality moves to a Gb^{11} chord, a tritone away from the previous root on C. The voices quickly descend and settle on a Bb tonal center on "Will write again." The sopranos take up the teletyping ostinato.

Figure 10-2. Jennifer Higdon, *Telegram*, mm. 10–15
Music Copyright © 2014 by Jennifer Higdon [ASCAP].
Poem by Jeanne Minahan (2012).

The next telegram goes in a new direction with its admonishing text, "Telegram from the Past: You left a paintbrush wet," and stern demand, "Send cash" (Figure 10-3). A secundal chord lands on the word "wet." There is a brief, dotted-eighth rest before the text "Send cash." The basses emphasize this demand by repeating it on a descending line in measure 20. The tonal center moves to C Mixolydian, with several $C^{7/9}$-type chords appearing in measures 19–21.

Figure 10-3. Jennifer Higdon, *Telegram*, pickup to mm. 18–21
Music Copyright © 2014 by Jennifer Higdon [ASCAP].
Poem by Jeanne Minahan (2012).

The succeeding "Telegram from the Future" states, "Now you have money. Bring paintbrush and more time." The first sentence is set in secundal chords, which could imaginatively be seen to represent stacks of money (Figure 10-4). In measure 25 on the word "time," a D major triad creates a new color, but two measures later this has flattened to D minor. The word "time" is stretched: it is set first on a half note amidst shorter rhythms, then repeated three times and the last time held for four beats, literally extending time. The basses now present a telegram-typing ostinato on open fifths, as a new telegram is about to come in.

Figure 10-4. Jennifer Higdon, *Telegram*, mm. 23–27
Music Copyright © 2014 by Jennifer Higdon [ASCAP].
Poem by Jeanne Minahan (2012).

This telegram is from, of all possibilities, a canary, who replies, apparently, to the question of how things are going (Figure 10-5). The canary chirps, "It's not bad, so far"—perhaps he has recently found a new home. The secundal writing continues, now grounded in the brighter harmony of D Dorian. The basses repeat the canary's answer as they hammer out a new message on the open fifth of D–A.

Figure 10-5. Jennifer Higdon, *Telegram*, mm. 29–33
Music Copyright © 2014 by Jennifer Higdon [ASCAP].
Poem by Jeanne Minahan (2012).

Coming out of the world of literature, Don Quixote's squire, Sancho Panza, sends the next message: "I'm starting to see things. Pack more wine." The music presents increased activity; the upper voices, SAT, move in ascending planing lines while the basses rise and fall in counterpoint. As Sancho says he is starting to "see things," surprise is expressed through the harmony, which moves a tritone away from the previous D center to an Ab root (Figure 10-6). The voices slide via glissandi while Sancho drunkenly requests "more wine," and the altos begin another telegram.

This message comes, tauntingly, from "my feet." The male voices in a very low range—a reference to the very bottom of the body—introduce the telegram. The sopranos and altos speak the message. They offer a brief admonishment, and remedy, from the sore feet: "Lighten up."

Figure 10-6. Jennifer Higdon, *Telegram*, mm. 36–41
Music Copyright © 2014 by Jennifer Higdon [ASCAP].
Poem by Jeanne Minahan (2012).

In the lofty "Telegram from the Sky," the men sing in parallel open fifths. Above the sustained male voices, the women's voices counter with the line "I'm the limit." The altos intermittently weave in the teletype's tapping.

The next section is expressed in an almost call and response style. The men are primarily in open fifths, and the women, set in counterpoint as a trio, cut in above the men's sustained chords. The men barely start the next message, "Telegram from Last Week…," when the women interrupt with "I can't catch up" (Figure 10-7). Continuing in the same string of eighth notes without any pause, all the voices sing, "and from Next [Week]." As the male voices are still finishing their line, the women lament, "and they won't let me wait." The men's voices are the delivery system for the telegram, while the women's voices illustrate, through their hurry and interruptions, the message about always rushing to catch up with time.

Figure 10-7. Jennifer Higdon, *Telegram*, mm. 44–48
Music Copyright © 2014 by Jennifer Higdon [ASCAP].
Poem by Jeanne Minahan (2012).

The next telegram continues on the theme of lost time and evokes a sentiment about which a good many people can likely relate: "Telegram smelling suspiciously of Rum and Coconut, from the Hour lost at the end of Daylight Savings Time. This time I'm not coming back."[1] In the midst of chordal homophony, contrary motion and dissonant stacked seconds occur on the word "suspiciously." The word is also highlighted by the use of B♮ in the midst of a passage full of B♭s. On the word "Time" in the phrase "the end of Daylight Savings Time" in measure 55 (Figure 10-8), the F major triad drops exactly one whole step to E♭ major, as if implying moving back one hour. When the telegram's author emphatically states, "This time, I'm not coming back," the choir rocks vigorously back and forth in parallel motion on E♭ and F major triads. They move to a surprising D major triad on the final word, "back." This new key represents a new start; harmonically, there is no "coming back." The altos and tenors mimic the clicking of the machine to bridge to the next telegram.

Figure 10-8. Jennifer Higdon, *Telegram*, mm. 53–57
Music Copyright © 2014 by Jennifer Higdon [ASCAP].
Poem by Jeanne Minahan (2012).

Descriptive harmonic colorations occur during the "Telegram from the Book left under the Covers: Do you read me?" The book is anxious about whether its owner will notice and read it, and its apprehension is expressed in harmonic instability. In particular, modal mixture occurs as C

---

[1]   It should be noted that Minahan's poem flips the concept of daylight savings time: an hour is gained, not lost, when daylight savings time ends. But Higdon has set the music in accordance with Minahan's poetry.

Mixolydian, with its B♭s, is juxtaposed with C Lydian, with its F♯s (Figure 10-9). There is a cross-relation of F♯ and F♮ between the bass and the alto parts in measure 59–60, followed by an unsettling alternation of F♯s and F♮s in the alto in measure 61. More instability is created as the measures of this passage alternate between 4/4 and 3/4 meter. The divisi tenors peck away on the teletype machine.

Figure 10-9. Jennifer Higdon, *Telegram*, mm. 59–62
Music Copyright © 2014 by Jennifer Higdon [ASCAP].
Poem by Jeanne Minahan (2012).

The next telegram refers to the ancient love affair of Cleopatra and Marc Antony but brings the romanticized story into the ordinariness of today by confirming Marc's health: "Telegram from Cleopatra: Marc's fine" (Figure 10-10). The music begins in F major, but the altos and basses continue their cross-relations of F to F♯. The altos continue with the F♯/F♮ alternation in the announcement "Boat race tomorrow." This cross-relation creates a degree of anxiety, subtly communicating Cleopatra's concern for Marc's wellbeing. The tenors, in divisi, continue to represent the teletype throughout this telegram.

Figure 10-10. Jennifer Higdon, *Telegram*, mm. 63–65
Music Copyright © 2014 by Jennifer Higdon [ASCAP].
Poem by Jeanne Minahan (2012).

In measure 66 the choir returns to homorhythm and appears to be approaching a peak. The text replies to two of the earlier telegrams: "Telegram to Last Week, I'll carry you with me. Telegram to Next Week: Wait." The texture intensifies through shorter rhythms of sixteenth and eighth notes. The ensemble moves in open fifths. As the chords rocket back and forth, the customary thirds and even added tones are absent, and the dynamic increases to *f*. In measures 66–70, the meter shifts with the poetic scansion: 4/4, two measures of 3/4, 2/4, and then 3/4 at the cadence (Figure 10-11). In measure 71, the word "Wait" is sustained and a major third is finally added. The typing resumes on the pitches D and G. This section moves downward harmonically, from roots of C to B♭ to A♭ and finally to G on the cadence at "Wait." Urgency is communicated through the diminished note values, changing meters, almost incessant open fifths for the full choir, and downward direction of each chord. Higdon ends with pointillistic offbeat entrances on the cautioning word "Wait." These delayed offbeat utterances give pause and symbolize the text.

Figure 10-11. Jennifer Higdon, *Telegram*, mm. 68–71
Music Copyright © 2014 by Jennifer Higdon [ASCAP].
Poem by Jeanne Minahan (2012).

The composition thins at this point. The female voices begin a new teletype ostinato duet, while the male voices announce a telegram from, of all entities, Elvis (Figure 10-12). He compliments the recipient's "nice shoes." Measure 74 contains an unresolved C$^{7/9}$ chord, a bluesy nod to Elvis.

The next telegram is a romantic "Telegram to your Lips" urging, "Kiss me." The C$^{7/9}$ chord for the Elvis cadence gives way to a G minor harmony in measure 75, but in the next measure, this rises to a hopeful G major triad on the word "lips." The imploring request "Kiss me" is crafted with a sliding glissando from a G major triad to an A major triad and a dynamic increase to f on a dotted-half note. It is a remarkable moment in mood painting; the listener feels the passion and hopeful anticipation in the request.

A fermata over a quarter rest denotes a pause in the score. Is this the kiss? The pause is unexpected and unprecedented in the otherwise constant rhythmic motion. Even the incessant tapping of the teletype machine stops as the audience is placed on a momentary hold.

Figure 10-12. Jennifer Higdon, *Telegram*, mm. 73–77
Music Copyright © 2014 by Jennifer Higdon [ASCAP].
Poem by Jeanne Minahan (2012).

After the romantic hiatus, the next section contains a reply to another previous message, "Telegram to the Hour from Daylight Savings Time." It spans seven measures that are surprisingly void of the tapping of the telegram, which does not reenter until measure 84 (Figure 10-13). The section moves in homorhythm. Harmonic ambiguities hint that things may not all be as hoped. The upper voices take the lead on the words "Smelling suspiciously of Rum and Coconut." The basses join on "Coconut," resolving to a D^9 chord—the same chord found in measure 51 when the telegram from daylight savings time was received. This recurring harmony affirms that Higdon connects tonal elements to particular concepts in the text. After just one beat, the D^9 chord moves into C Lydian through a double suspension (F♯–D moves to E–C) on the words "Flight booked." The music conveys the sender's urgency and impatience; the sender is less than reassured of the recipient's faithfulness, given the suspicious fragrance of the telegram. All the voices state in an emphatic eighth-note rhythm, "Joining you next week." The notes ascend rapidly in an accelerando.

Both this telegram and the "Telegram to your lips" demonstrate Higdon's attention to poetic scansion and rhythmic articulations. The counterpoint between voices never obscures the natural inflections of the text. The text is kept understandable through the rhythmic sculpting of stressed and unstressed syllables. When meters change within a given line, the natural scansion of the text is respected. Elongated rhythmic values are used to emphasize pertinent words in the text—for example, the word "wait" in measure 70 of Figure 10-11, the words "kiss" and "me" in measures 76–77 of Figure 10-12, and the word "week" in measure 84 of Figure 10-13. Higdon elongates these words to create the impression of elongating time, as we "wait" or enjoy a "kiss," especially a kiss with "me," and as we anticipate the length of a "week."

Figure 10-13. Jennifer Higdon, *Telegram*, mm. 80–84.
Music Copyright © 2014 by Jennifer Higdon [ASCAP].
Poem by Jeanne Minahan (2012).

The "dot, dot" syllables of the inner voices push onward to the next telegram. The new message is delivered with exasperation and interruptions: "Telegram … from the Telegraph … Office: …" (the ellipses represent rests in the music). The irritated sender tells the recipient, "Buy yourself a cell phone." Minahan is, of course, being teasing by mentioning cellphones during the age of telegrams. The male voices sing on the offbeats in counterpoint against the female voices to underscore the sender's frustration. The use of syncopated rhythms, set in the context of consistent eighth notes in the female voices, creates an anxious tension and reveals annoyance that the telegram's recipient does not yet have a cell phone!

As with the setting of the word "wait" in measure 70 in Figure 10-11, Higdon uses offbeats to make a dramatic point. A measure in 2/4 meter is added, granting the male voices an opportunity to continue berating the recipient for lacking modern technology. Higdon portrays the telegram's author muttering, repeating the word "phone" on a diminuendo. This is sung on alternating beats in measures 88–89 (Figure 10-14a).

Figure 10-14a. Jennifer Higdon, *Telegram*, mm. 88–89
Music Copyright © 2014 by Jennifer Higdon [ASCAP].
Poem by Jeanne Minahan (2012).

Silence is now demanded in the "Telegram from the Library." Harmonic colorations coupled with carefully placed rhythmic pauses convey the librarian's stern warning. The harmony moves from the E♭ major of the previous telegram, to D♭ major and then a more somber D minor for the directive to "Silence, please" (Figure 10-14b). A dramatic pause occurs over two beats before the singing of "Silence, please" in ***pp***, and another pause is inserted between these two words.

Figure 10-14b. Jennifer Higdon, *Telegram*, mm. 90–93
Music Copyright © 2014 by Jennifer Higdon [ASCAP].
Poem by Jeanne Minahan (2012).

A grand pause follows, allowing quiet in the library. The respite from telegram typing generates anticipation for what might come next.

The new telegram is "to the President." Its relatively slower rhythmic values—eighth notes, quarter notes, and dotted-half notes, as opposed to the eighth and sixteenth notes of the surrounding passages—convey gravitas (Figure 10-15). The word "President" is accordingly sustained over four beats. The sopranos ascend a full octave in this phrase, which is the largest expansion in the melody thus far. The message to the president is "Peace." With this request, the sopranos retrace their scale downward. The internal voices utter the word "peace" three times in subtly interrupted entrances that sound like breathless pleas. The basses delay the final chord and rise slowly to their final note, signaling both hope and entreaty. The phrase ends without resolution. There is no assurance that the president will honor the request.

Figure 10-15. Jennifer Higdon, *Telegram*, mm. 95–98
Music Copyright © 2014 by Jennifer Higdon [ASCAP].
Poem by Jeanne Minahan (2012).

The mood becomes lighter and the music lyrical as a telegram is sent to Emily Dickinson. The three upper voices deliver a gentle ascending line spanning an octave and starting on the Eb borrowed from the previous cadence (Figure 10-16). This line initially sounds as Eb Mixolydian with the indicative Dbs, but cross-relations with D♮s soon appear. This synthetic scale provides an uplifting, hopeful effect. Singing "We quote you now," the female voices, representing the poet, move into triadic formulas in SSA. The next phrase is incomplete: "Roses, Bees, but Yours the Nectar, yours the—." The tenors sing "Roses," echoed by the female voices. The basses sing "Bees," again echoed in the female voices. The voices musically buzz in beating harmonic seconds. Added notes, seconds, and fourths abound. For example, "Yours the nectar" is built on stacked seconds, grounded in a Db tonal center that moves stepwise downward. The unfinished phrase drops off, interrupted by the typing of another telegram. All the voice parts erupt into teletyping dots and dashes for the only time in the composition. Shifting accents and offbeat utterances gather momentum for what appears to be the closing portion of the work.

Figure 10-16. Jennifer Higdon, *Telegram*, mm. 99–101 and mm. 104–105
Music Copyright © 2014 by Jennifer Higdon [ASCAP].
Poem by Jeanne Minahan (2012).

The sound of the teletype hammers away in a bridge over measures 105–109 (Figure 10-17). Measures 107–109 emphatically strike a series of quarter note chords marked *f* and *marcato*. The choir here spells out the actual Morse code for the word "God"—G: "Dash, Dash, dot," O: "Dash, Dash, Dash," and D: "Dash, dot, dot." God is the recipient of the coming telegram. Higdon remarks: "I've always been fascinated by Morse code, and the use of it here seemed fitting for the text and in particular for the God section."[2]

Figure 10-17. Jennifer Higdon, *Telegram*, mm. 105–109
Music Copyright © 2014 by Jennifer Higdon [ASCAP].
Poem by Jeanne Minahan (2012).

The "Telegram to God" is the high point of the work, its text is delivered in *ff* (Figure 10-18). The telegram's content is "Message received." Secundal chords are found on "Message," while "received" is elongated. The altos' dots and dashes overlap as another telegram is transmitted.

2   Jennifer Higdon, email to the author, August 12, 2020.

Figure 10-18. Jennifer Higdon, *Telegram*, mm. 110–114
Music Copyright © 2014 by Jennifer Higdon [ASCAP].
Poem by Jeanne Minahan (2012).

The last four telegrams are from the four seasons. For the "Telegram from Summer," the tenors and sopranos enter in *mp*, in contrast to the previous *ff* (Figure 10-18). They ask, "Have you forgotten me?" The altos type away on the pitch F.

The altos' typing then lowers by a whole step to E♭. All voices continue in this tonal center for the "Telegram from Fall." Wordplay is used in the poetry, "I've changed," while the harmony coincidingly changes, downward a step to D♭ (Figure 10-19). The tenors, in a wonderful moment of word painting, repeat the word "change" four times. Their repetitive urging is echo-like, indicating that, as the season has changed, the sender of the telegram has changed too, over time. With the repetition, the sender pleads with the recipient to believe them.

Winter follows immediately: "Telegram from Winter: Be there, soon." The choir sings in light counterpoint, with the tenors weaving among the other voices. The harmonic motion moves downward, E♭–D♭–C, repeating in diminution the tonal progression used over the last three telegrams. On the text "Be there, soon," the male voices ascend in a B♭ Lydian scale to the final telegram.

Figure 10-19. Jennifer Higdon, *Telegram*, mm. 117–122
Music Copyright © 2014 by Jennifer Higdon [ASCAP].
Poem by Jeanne Minahan (2012).

The final telegram is the "Telegram from Hope: Spring's eternal" (Figure 10-20). Minahan has adjusted the aphorism "Hope springs eternal" to fit it with the theme of the seasons. Tonally, the piece is back where it began, C Lydian. The rhythms are now longer, and there are no more dots, dashes, or ostinatos. The tempo is slowed to 72 for the quarter note, down from the previous 104 marking. Further stretching the note values, "Hope" is set on a half note and "Spring's" on a dotted quarter. For four measures at the end, the last syllable of "eternal" is sustained. The C Lydian settles on a C major triad for the cadence, which occurs on the second beat rather than on the usual downbeat. The basses move from the chord's third to its root in the final measure, marked with a fermata. "Hope" is indeed meant to spring eternally, as the rhythmic values augment, elongate, and fade.

Figure 10-20. Jennifer Higdon, *Telegram*, mm. 123–129
Music Copyright © 2014 by Jennifer Higdon [ASCAP].
Poem by Jeanne Minahan (2012).

Each concise telegram is fitted to a creative and custom-designed musical setting, yet there is coherence and organic continuity. After having spent over forty years conducting choral works from every period, works large and small, I know of very few pieces like *Telegram*. With its rapidly shifting colors, textures, and tonal centers, *Telegram* is wonderfully challenging to perform and has become a favorite of the choirs under my direction. Because of its use of varying texts and musical formulas, *Telegram* illustrates the craft of Higdon's music–text interactions and many of the tonal and technique elements in her choral works.

CHAPTER ELEVEN

ANALYTICAL SUMMARY

Higdon is both a lifelong student and a master of composition. She walks in the footsteps of generations of composers and honors their musical traditions in her works. Her innovative and diverse musical palate gives the classical tradition a fresh voice that speaks to a twenty-first-century audience.

To summarize the techniques in any significant composer's works is a daunting task, one that is fraught from the start with the challenges of dissecting a number of sophisticated compositions, scrutinizing a wealth of complex information, analyzing individual excerpts, and deducing how they interact with their texts. The intention in this chapter is not to over-simplify Higdon's stylistic traits and tendencies; rather, it is to give her writing the serious attention it deserves and to enlighten and draw readers into her works.

Any analysis of music in relation to text is inherently subjective and will be perceived differently by different scholars and performers. Music will also be received differently by each audience member. In short, there is no one size will fit all when discussing an artistic subject. Aware of these conditions, this author has scrutinized Higdon's music and offered conclusions based on a thorough assessment of patterns in her compositions. What is presented here is based on sound music theory and musical and poetic analyses; it is critically thought through, detailed, and current with regards to contemporary musical analysis.

Structure and Text

Whether Higdon selects a text by herself or agrees to one selected by someone else for a commission, the text must fit her compositional style and taste. She has explained the need for a text to align with her personal instincts:

If the text doesn't resonate with me, how can I expect to write a convincing work that the audience can relate to? If I don't connect with a text, I think listeners would hear a kind of insincerity come through.[1]

Higdon's choral repertoire reveals that she is a serious person of dramatic, emotional, social, and artistic depth. Flippant or shallow texts are rare in her oeuvre. Among the works collected in this volume demonstrating this depth, are the poems by Jeanne Minahan and Paul Lawrence Dunbar, a sermon by John Donne, writings by Rumi, the libretto for *Cold Mountain*, and Higdon's own text included in *Alleluia*. A few texts are less serious, but even in such cases, Higdon develops a complexity of musical thought that elicits respect and gives the songs an unexpected profundity. Examples include the upbeat and folk-like pieces in *Southern Grace*, such as "Fiddlin'" and "Swing." As another example, one will rarely find more humorous and ironic texts than those in *Telegram*, which are by Minahan, the same author of the spiritual poetry contained in *The Singing Rooms*. Even in its lighter sections, *Telegram* is threaded with social, political, and spiritual overtones. Higdon presents poignant messages that allude to social justice, psychological and religious issues, and contemplative notions about society and humanity.

Higdon coordinates the structure of her music and the structure of the text hand-in-hand. She adapts, edits, interrupts, truncates, or repeats lines of poetry to emphasize the text's attributes. Phrases or quatrains of poetry correspond with units of music. Repetitions of a text or concept are often found with recurring musical ideas, such as a motive or tonality. For example, a key or chord will be used to recall a poetic phrase or similar poetic concept. The end of a section of poetry is marked by a cadence, but often a new section of music and text will overlap this cadence and keep the composition moving and the audience engaged.

Pieces often begin with just a few words or syllables from the poem, to which Higdon gradually adds a word or a syllable at a time. This method of text adaptation builds suspense and interest as the text unfolds. It is used in "Swing" when the men sing the word "swing" for a few measures before the first verse begins. In "The Fox," from the same collection, nonsense syllables evoke the energy of a fox on the hunt, before the audience learns what is happening. Other instances occur in the broken and rhythmic syllables in *Alleluia*, the solemn opening of *O magnum mysterium*, the ethereal entrance of *The Singing Rooms*, and the early church, chant-like introduction of *On the Death of the Righteous*. Whether a piece is

---

[1]   Jennifer Higdon, email to the author, March 31, 2020.

accompanied or a cappella, Higdon creates a mood through instrumental or vocal sounds before offering a substantial amount of text.

The atmosphere from a work's beginning typically returns at the end. This structural framing is seen in *The Singing Rooms*, *On the Death of the Righteous*, *Our Beautiful Country*, and *O magnum mysterium*, where significant portions of similar music begin and end the work. Even short songs such as "Fiddlin'" and "Swing" contain this structure in a miniaturized form.

Higdon often writes several high points per work. These usually build consecutively to an ultimate climax late in the piece and before a more relaxed section. Such moments are found in "Amazing Grace," "Wildwood Flower," *O magnum mysterium*, *The Singing Rooms*, and *On the Death of the Righteous*. Other times the climax ends the piece and the listener is left with a satisfying final exclamation point as in "The Fox," "Swing," and *Ruminations*. Climaxes occur as shorter units in small-form compositions and as longer units over several measures in the larger works. In virtually every case, the structural high points correspond with important moments in the text.

Instrumentation and Orchestration

As Higdon is internationally acclaimed for her instrumental writing, it comes as no surprise that her choral works accompanied by orchestra also display her instrumental prowess. Profound and adventurous orchestrations are found throughout the works for full orchestra. *The Singing Rooms*, which is essentially a violin concerto with chorus, was written on the heels of the violin concerto that won her the Pulitzer Prize. *On the Death of the Righteous* was scored with similar instrumentation as Verdi's *Requiem*. *Ruminations* was written for a chamber orchestra; the twelve solo players offer transparent, expressive, even virtuoso instrumentals.

During the choral portions in these orchestrated works, a great deal of sensitivity and care is exercised, as the orchestra rarely, if ever, doubles the choir. The choir's lines are most often independent of the orchestral passages yet are heard in close relationship with them. The orchestration is thin so that the poetry remains clear. When a large chorus is singing and repeats a text, the instrumentation is then allowed to take on more demanding contemporary musical idioms. And when the voices are absent in the sometimes lengthy interludes that bridge phrases of text and at cadences, the orchestration is its thickest and most sophisticated.

Whether the instruments are fully scored or thinly veiled, Higdon's instrumentation is crafted to suit the mood and the meaning of the text. In *On the Death of the Righteous* the chimes ring in a weaving, descant-like counterpoint above the choir, creating an ethereal, traditional church-like atmosphere. Similarly, in *O magnum mysterium* crystal glasses, flutes, and chimes provide austere and archaic sounds floating over and around the vocal lines. *The Singing Rooms* is marked by tour-de-force violin solos that represent a soul traveling through the rooms of life. The instruments play roles in these music-dramas and give life to the text. Throughout Higdon's compositions, the orchestration is carefully crafted to support the singers in a quasi-art-song fashion, much like a piano accompaniment in a Schumann lied.

Counterpoint and Vocal Textures

Higdon writes intelligently for voices and is sensitive to inherent vocal and aural challenges. She is demanding, but adapts to what the singers can effectively express; in some cases, this is different from what she asks from the instrumentalists.

Textural choices available to Higdon include vocal timbres, polyphony, homophony, chordal, unison, and divisi writing. Voicings are used to create musical conversations that embody the character of the words. For example, female versus male voicings often deliver texts that relate to traditional male and female notions. Inner versus outer vocal parts also depict the text in conversational ways. Voices are often set in pairs against one another or set as one voice against the others. Such arrangements can use imitation or contrasting themes.

Beginning a phrase in unison is common and grants the text clarity and transparency. Sometimes a melody begins in unison on the first word or words, but expands vertically and horizontally with added text. As the voices gradually branch into added layers, they create a secundal, added tone texture.

Complex counterpoint and divisi textures are most frequently used after a text has been introduced, so as not to obscure it, and in the buildup to climaxes. Such sections normally use imitative, stretto-like techniques that build until a homophonic climax. Sometimes the reverse occurs, and homophony and chordal planing develop into a contrapuntal setting. These instances significantly change the character of the piece, dramatizing that moment. This hallmark in Higdon's choral music is especially seen in the larger works such as *The Singing Rooms*, *On the Death of the Righteous*, and *Ruminations*.

Counterpoint can also symbolize the meaning of a text, as in the jubilant lines in *Alleluia* and the folk-like independent melodic lines in "Fiddlin'," "Swing," and "Sourwood Mountain." In "Amazing Grace" creative counterpoint gives new depth to the traditional hymn text. In *O magnum mysterium* an organum-like setting is created beneath the main melodic theme. In *Invitation to Love*, the altos' delayed entrances and resolutions imitate a bird alighting in its nest. The refined counterpoint in Higdon's choral music portrays elements of poetry, adds impact, incites interest, and is often subliminal.

Melody

With the exception of the folk-like themes in *Southern Grace*, including "Wildwood Flower," "My True Love's Hair," and "Amazing Grace," Higdon writes few melodies that one might sing on one's way home from a concert. Her melodies are rather intended to illuminate a given text and enhance its drama. The melodic designs defy a one-size-fits-all description, but there are some consistencies in how she creates melodic contours and motives.

In one type of motivic creation, a fairly short melodic unit begins and then repeats in gradually expanding range, contour, and length. Melodies like this evolve as text is added, building interest while the listener waits for an entire line to be knit together. This type of melody often combines with the texture described above in which one voice begins with a fragment and other voices layer in succession. In these cases, melody takes a back seat to texture and harmony. The motive will undergo gradual alterations, sometimes coupled with rhythmic metamorphoses or expanded intervallic techniques.

A number of melodies in Higdon's choral works are more linear. These are broader and lengthier from the start and are often constructed in an arched contour. Melodies like this serve as the foundation for works such as *Our Beautiful Country*, *Invitation to Love*, "Wildwood Flower," and "My True Love's Hair." These lyric melodies fall on the ear with a lush warmth and are inspired by a certain type of poetry; in *Invitation to Love*, for example, the arched and consonant melodies express the warm embrace of the title.

Other melodies are shaped into continuous ascending and descending contours. Portions of *The Singing Rooms* contain such melodies, like the setting of the Irish proverb near the end, "Your feet will bring you to where your heart is."

Some melodies are intended to represent a specific traditional element. In *On the Death of the Righteous* and *O magnum mysterium*, the themes imitate chant. These narrow and stepwise melodies convey reverence through their association with medieval sacred music. Other motivic constructions represent instruments, as found in the open-string tuning of a violin imitated in *The Singing Rooms*. In *Southern Grace*, the melodies in "Fiddlin'" copy idiomatic Southern fiddle-style melodies, and the voices in "Sourwood Mountain" take on a banjo's rhythmic articulations.

Overall melodic design is consistently and meaningfully wedded to the text. It is unique to each piece and fits each poem, each phrase, each mood.

Rhythm and Meter

In her vocal writing, Higdon observes naturally stressed and unstressed syllables to respect the natural scansion and articulation of the text. Rhythmic values are adjusted by augmentation and diminution to enhance the text. Diminishing rhythmic values and tightening rhythmic structures create forward motion or urgency, while augmenting rhythmic values give the poetry added breadth and gravitas.

Broken, fragmented rhythmic motives, sometimes in pointillistic voice-exchange, create anticipation. Such instances occur at the end of *Invitation to Love* and *O magnum mysterium*, and are a defining characteristic in *Alleluia*.

Changing and asymmetrical meters are less common in Higdon's choral works than in her instrumental pieces. In the choral works, traditional duple and triple meters (simple and compound) are most common and provide stability for the text delivery. When changing and asymmetrical meters do appear, it is usually to accommodate the text's natural scansion or to provide variation in purely instrumental portions. Sometimes a text is offered initially in a more traditional meter, and then repeated as the meter is altered to truncate or expand the poetic phrase. In sections that contain several changes of meter or asymmetrical meters, these choices are aimed to dramatize the poetry or aid text enunciation and emphasis.

Harmony

The harmonic work in Higdon's choral writing is grounded in traditional thought, yet delivered with a fresh contemporary voice. Though at its core it is tonal, it is also innovative and unpredictable. She excels in shifting tonal centers and using synthetic modes outside the traditional modal system. Her inner ear determines what harmony to craft, always in consort with the text.

Higdon mixes traditional scales and modes by starting in one mode and continuing in another. Unpredictable harmonic moments align with texts that convey discord, controversy, or, conversely, euphoria. One synthetic scale used often in the works analyzed here uses the first four notes of a Lydian scale and the last four notes of Mixolydian. Another common harmonic element is an unanticipated switch from one tonality to another after a cadence. The new and unexpected color captures the listener's attention. Such changes correlate with new sections of poetry, as in *Telegram* and *Invitation to Love*. Root movements by thirds are also common, especially when associated with poetry that is uplifting and hopeful.

Higdon chooses harmonies to highlight syllables, words, complete phrases, or entire sections of music. The harmonic rhythm is typically rapid, though static harmonies accompany certain texts. Extended chords and added-tone chords create sustained tonal atmospheres that augment dramatic character.

Polychords and polytonal allusions occur on occasion, especially when approaching climactic cadence points. These thick, colorful, and emphatic harmonies illuminate texts aligned with high drama. The clearest examples are found in large-form works such as *The Singing Rooms* and *On the Death of the Righteous*, but they occur as well in some of the smaller works. "Amazing Grace," *O magnum mysterium*, *Invitation to Love*, and *Alleluia* all contain polychordal harmonies.

Another harmonic technique used especially when building to cadential high points is chordal parallelism. The approach to a peak is intensified by the harmonic gathering of forces through parallel motion. This planing, normally contained in the entire choir, is sometimes doubled in the orchestra or occurs in orchestral counterpoint beneath the choir. These motions emphasize the text in impactful ways. In *The Singing Rooms* and *On the Death of the Righteous*, the full chorus and orchestra use planing to create overwhelming moments for an audience.

Octatonicism is used on occasion in the instrumentation and rarely in the vocals, but such nomenclature has been largely left out of this book. It tends to last for only a measure or a portion of a measure. When asked about her use of octatonicism, Higdon wrote:

> I have never once thought about whether a line was octatonic or not. I used to teach the use of these scales in other people's works when I taught twentieth-century music theory and history at Curtis Institute of Music, but

that was the last time I consciously thought about these scales. The knowledge of them exists in my head, but when it comes to composing, I never plan these things out and wouldn't know that they're even there.[2]

While modern harmonies and scales flavor Higdon's writing as contemporary, some of her works convey eclectic styles connecting disparate centuries. Open fifths throughout *On the Death of the Righteous* and *O magnum mysterium* reinforce the chant-like melodies and evoke medieval harmonic practices of the twelfth and thirteenth centuries. In other cases, harmonic idioms are associated with specific instrumentation: in the open fourths and fifths in "Fiddlin'," "Swing," and *The Singing Rooms*, the choir metaphorically becomes the tuning strings of folk instruments and the violin. In "Sourwood Mountain," the voices sing the banjo's tuning notes.

In her most complex works, Higdon creates a home tone or home chord. Regardless of a work's complexities, and perhaps sometimes because of them, this comforting chord becomes a point of harmonic rest. In the midst of tonal ambiguities, a home chord—normally coupled with words that are core in a work's message—returns as a tonal center, anchoring those critical points in time. The home chord also acts to unify the work, going beyond the traditional sense of a piece being in one key. G major returns throughout *The Singing Rooms*, while A major becomes a home chord in *On the Death of the Righteous*. A♭ and B major are grounding points in *Our Beautiful Country*, while D major anchors *O magnum mysterium*, though other tonal centers emerge throughout the piece.

Higdon speaks through her powerful musical voice in the many stylistic traits discussed here and throughout this book. Her compositions can be likened to the pieces of a great painter. How the techniques are used can be assessed, how they are combined can be analyzed, but their overall impact is ultimately attributable to the painter's inner instincts: their inner eye, or, in this case, her inner ear.

---

[2]   Jennifer Higdon, email to the author, November 17, 2020.

CHAPTER TWELVE

FINAL THOUGHTS

Jennifer Higdon is a prolific composer of choral works that, to date, live in relative obscurity. Part of the goal in this book has been to introduce these works to musicians, scholars, poets, and music appreciators. The compositions analyzed here were selected from her ever-growing choral output, which is listed in its current totality in the appendix. Given the depth of musical and poetic thought in Higdon's compositions, hundreds of additional musical examples could have been included. It is hoped that this offering will inspire continued interest in her works. This volume is not intended to be the final word: there is much more to be said.

The pieces discussed here are representative of Higdon's choral output and demonstrate that each musical component—whether melody, harmony, rhythm, structure, texture, instrumentation, or voicing—can be inspired by the text. The many innovative ways that Higdon sets text are indeed part of the reason her music can speak profoundly to an audience. This music is engaging because each element appears intricately conceived in connection to the text.

As demonstrated in the theoretical analyses in this book, Higdon's works are more complex than they may at first sound. That is part of her gift, and for the performers, it is part of their challenge. The choral music is as complex as her other genres of composition. It reveals a sophisticated musical ear and the same high level of artistic sensitivity found in her numerous award-winning and commissioned orchestral compositions. One difference is that, in her choral music, her already dense compositional process is given another layer through the added element of text setting. As each text uniquely drives her musical choices, the diversity of texts makes each piece an original, though all are decidedly Higdon.

Why *Choral Kaleidoscope*? Higdon's choral writing displays a wide array of colors: structure, melody, harmony, counterpoint, rhythm, instrumentation, and the overall aesthetic express a diverse palate of musical hues. Her works are truly a composite image of meticulously crafted individual elements. Their beauty speaks intimately and directly. It is hoped this discussion will entice others to explore Higdon's choral music more deeply through listening, studying, and performance. Her music is worthy of this attention.

Appendix

Alphabetical List of Jennifer Higdon's Choral Works

Sacred/Secular	Secular	Sacred/Christmas	Secular Pub.: Hal Leonard	Secular	Sacred/Christmas	Sacred/Christmas
Duration	4 minutes	6 minutes	4 minutes	4 minutes	4 minutes	6 minutes
Text by	Jennifer Higdon	Jennifer Higdon	Jennifer Higdon	Paul Laurence Dunbar for Ann Meier Baker	Christina Rossetti	Sacred
Scoring	SATB chorus a cappella	SATB chorus a cappella	3-part mixed chorus Piano	SATB chorus a cappella	Solo soprano SATB chorus Harp	*Version A:* SATB chorus 2 flutes, 2 crystal glasses, chimes *Version B:* SATB chorus Organ *Version C:* SATB chorus a cappella
Title	*Alleluia* 2016	*Deep in the Night* 1997	*Hear My Voice*	*Invitation to Love* 2016	*Love Came Down* 2015	*O magnum mysterium* 2002

Alphabetical List of Jennifer Higdon's Choral Works

Sacred/Secular	Secular	Secular/patriotic	Spiritual	Spiritual
Duration	12 minutes	3 minutes 30 seconds	3 minutes	17 minutes
Text by	John Donne	Gene Scheer	Jennifer Higdon In memory of Andrew Blue Higdon	Rumi Translation by Coleman Barks
Scoring	SATB chorus Orchestra: 3 (3rd also picc.), 2, 2, 4, 4, 5, 3 picc. trpt., 3, 3, 1, timp., 1 perc., strings	TTBB chorus	*Version A:* TTBB chorus *Version B:* SSAA chorus *Version C:* SATB chorus a cappella	SATB chorus Chamber ensemble (total of 12 players) 1, 1 (doubling bass clarinet), 1, 1, 1, hp, 1 perc., 2 violins, 1 viola, 1 cello, 1 contrabass
Title	*On the Death of the Righteous* 2008	*Our Beautiful Country* 2015 (from the opera, Cold Mountain, Act II)	*A Quiet Moment* 1999	*Ruminations* 2016

Appendix

Sacred/Secular	Sacred	Spiritual/Christmas (universal)	Secular/spiritual	Secular
Duration	4 minutes	3 minutes	37 minutes	5 minutes
Text by	Sacred	Jennifer Higdon	Jeanne Minahan	e.e. cummings
Scoring	SSAATTBB chorus a cappella,	SATB chorus a cappella	Solo violin SATB chorus Orchestra: 2, 2 (2nd also Eng. hn.) 2, 2, 4, 3 (1st also picc. tpt.), 3, 1 hp., timp, 2 perc., strings	SATB chorus Piano, Vibraphone
Title	*Sanctus* 2001	*Sing, Sing* 1999	*The Singing Rooms* 2007	*somewhere i have never traveled, gladly beyond* 2006

Alphabetical List of Jennifer Higdon's Choral Works

Sacred/ Secular	Seven secular, one sacred	Secular	Secular	Secular	Secular	Secular	Secular	Secular
Duration	24 minutes	2 minutes	3 minutes	2 minutes	3 minutes	1 minute 42 seconds	2–3 minutes	2 minutes
Text by	Collection of eight songs	Solfège text	Folk poetry	Folk poetry	Folk poetry	Folk poetry	Folk song: "I Gave My Love a Cherry"	Folk poetry
Scoring	SATB, SSAA, and TTBB chorus Solo quartet a cappella	SATB chorus	SATB chorus	SATB chorus a cappella	SSAA chorus	SATB chorus	SSAATTBB chorus a cappella	*Version A:* SATB chorus *Version B:* TTBB chorus
Title	**Southern Grace** 1998	**Fiddlin'**	**Wildwood Flower**	**Swing**	**My True Love's Hair**	**The Fox**	**Riddle Song**	**Sourwood Mountain**

Appendix

Sacred/Secular	Sacred	Secular	Secular	Secular/patriotic
Duration	7 minutes	6 minutes	4 minutes	3 minutes
Text by	Hymn	Jeanne Minahan	William Blake	Gene Scheer
Scoring	*Version A:* SATB chorus *Version B:* TTBB chorus	SATB chorus a cappella	TTBB chorus a cappella	*Version A:* TBB & Piano *Version B:* Solo soprano Solo alto TTBB chorus
Title	*Southern Grace* (continued)	**Amazing Grace**	***Telegram*** 2014	***Voice of the Bard*** 2005	***What Was His Name?*** 2015 (from the opera **Cold Mountain**, Act I)

Ordering information:

Unless otherwise noted, all works are published by Lawdon Press

Order by email: Lawdonpress@aol.com

Website: www.jenniferhigdon.com